# TRAVELING MERCIES

*Also by* ANNE LAMOTT

# ANNE LAMOTT

# TRAVELING MERCIES

*Some Thoughts on Faith*

*Pantheon Books*

NEW YORK

Portions of this work were originally published in different
form in Salon Magazine.

Permissions Acknowledgments appear on page 274.

Library of Congress Cataloging-in-Publication Data

Lamott, Anne.
Traveling mercies : some thoughts on faith / Anne Lamott.
p.        cm.
ISBN 0-679-44240-5
1. Lamott, Anne—Religion.    2. Women novelists, American—
20th century—Biography.    3. Christian biography—United
States.    4. Mothers and sons—United States.    5. Faith.
I. Title.
PS3562.A4645Z47   1999
813'.54—dc21
[B]        98-30487
CIP

Random House Web Address: www.randomhouse.com

Book design by M. Kristen Bearse

Printed in the United States of America

8    9    7

*This is dedicated to the people of*
*St. Andrew Presbyterian Church,*
*Marin City, California*
*The Reverend Ms. Veronica Goines, pastor*

*and to Father Tom Weston, S.J.*

Listen
with the night falling we are saying thank you
we are stopping on the bridge to bow from the railings
we are running out of the glass rooms
with our mouths full of food to look at the sky
and say thank you
we are standing by the water looking out
in different directions

back from a series of hospitals back from a mugging
after funerals we are saying thank you
after the news of the dead
whether or not we knew them we are saying thank you
in a culture up to its chin in shame
living in the stench it has chosen we are saying thank you

over telephones we are saying thank you
in doorways and in the backs of cars and in elevators
remembering wars and the police at the back door
and the beatings on stairs we are saying thank you

in the banks that use us we are saying thank you
with the crooks in office with the rich and fashionable
unchanged we go on saying thank you thank you

with the animals dying around us
our lost feelings we are saying thank you
with the forests falling faster than the minutes
of our lives we are saying thank you
with the words going out like cells of a brain
with the cities growing over us like the earth
we are saying thank you faster and faster
with nobody listening we are saying thank you
we are saying thank you and waving
dark though it is

—W. S. MERWIN

# CONTENTS

# CONTENTS

# TRAVELING MERCIES

# OVERTURE:
# LILY PADS

My coming to faith did not start with a leap but rather a series of staggers from what seemed like one safe place to another. Like lily pads, round and green, these places summoned and then held me up while I grew. Each prepared me for the next leaf on which I would land, and in this way I moved across the swamp of doubt and fear. When I look back at some of these early resting places—the boisterous home of the Catholics, the soft armchair of the Christian Science mom, adoption by ardent Jews—I can see how flimsy and indirect a path they made. Yet each step brought me closer to the verdant pad of faith on which I somehow stay afloat today.

### That One Ridiculous Palm

The railroad yard below our house was ringed in green, in grass and weeds and blackberry bushes and shoulder-high anise plants that smelled and tasted of licorice; this wreath of green, like a cell membrane, contained the tracks and the trains and the roundhouse, where engines were repaired. The buildings rose up out of the water on the other side of the bay, past Angel Island, past Alcatraz. You could see the Golden Gate Bridge over to the right behind Belvedere, where the richer people lived; the anise was said to have been brought over at the turn of the century by the Italians who gardened for the people of Belvedere.

Tiburon, where I grew up, used to be a working-class town where the trains still ran. Now mostly wealthy people live here. It means shark in Spanish, and there are small sharks in these parts. My father and shy Japanese fishermen used to catch leopard sharks in the cold green waters of the bay.

There was one palm tree at the western edge of the rail-road yard, next to the stucco building of the superinten-dent—one tall incongruous palm tree that we kids thought was very glamorous but that the grown-ups referred to as "that ridiculous palm tree." It did not belong, was not in relationship to anything else in town. It was silent and comical, like Harpo Marx with a crazy hat of fronds.

We took our underpants off for older boys behind the blackberry bushes. They'd give us things—baseball cards, Sugar Babies. We chewed the stems off the anise plants and sucked on them, bit the ends off nasturtiums and drank the nectar.

When I was five and six, my best friend was a Catholic girl who lived about fifteen minutes away, on foot, from our house—kids walked alone all over town back then. I loved the Catholic family desperately. There were dozens of children in that family, or maybe it just felt that way, babies everywhere, babies crawling out from under sofas like dust bunnies. We only had three kids in our family; my brother John, who is two years older than me and didn't like me very much back then, and my brother Stevo, who is five years younger than me, whom I always adored, and who always loved me. My mother nursed him discreetly, while the Catholic mother wore each new baby on her breasts like a brooch. The Catholic mama was tall and gorgeous and wore heels to church and lots of makeup, like Sophia Loren, and she had big bosoms that she showed off in stylish V-necked dresses from the Sears catalog. My mother was not much of a dresser. Also, she was short, and did not believe in God. She was very political, though; both she and Dad were active early on in the civil rights movement. My parents and all their friends were yellow-dog Democrats, which is to say that they would have voted for an old yellow dog before they would have voted for a Republican.

I was raised by my parents to believe that you had a moral obligation to try to save the world. You sent money to the Red Cross, you registered people to vote, you marched in rallies, stood in vigils, picked up litter. My mother used to take the Greyhound out to Marin City, which was a terrible ghetto then, and volunteer in an after-school program for boys and girls from impoverished families. She tutored kids in reading while other grown-ups worked with them in sports. My mother majored in the classics in college. She always brought along little paper candy cups filled with the fanciest candies from Blum's or the City of Paris to give to the children after their lessons. It used to make my father mad that she'd buy such expensive candies, but this didn't stop her.

My Catholic friend and I used to spend hours sitting on the couch with the latest Sears catalog spread across our knees, pretending that we got whatever was on our side of the page. I played this game with anxiety and grief, always thinking that the better dresses and shoes were on my friend's pages and that I would have been OK if they had just been on mine—*and* if I'd had her tall stylish mother, with the wonderful cleavage showing like the bottom of a baby in her low necklines. I knew I was not pretty because people were always making jokes about my looks. (Once, at a pizza joint, a stranger had included me in a collective reference to the Catholic children, and you would have thought from the parents' outrage that he had included a chimpanzee.) And I knew I was not OK because I got teased a lot by strangers or by big boys for having hair that was fuzzy and white. Also, I got migraines. I got my first one midway through kindergarten and had to lie down with my face on the cool linoleum in the back of the room until my father could come get me.

My friend and I gathered blackberries from the bushes in the train yard, and her mother made pies. She made apple pies too. We peeled each apple with precision, aiming for one long green spiral of peel, and my first memory of watching someone be beaten was on a night after we'd prepared apples for pie. My Catholic friend and I had been left with a baby-sitter and all those babies, and after we had sliced up and spiced the apples, we'd gone to bed without throwing out all those green snakes of peel, and I awoke with a start in the middle of the night because my friend's father was smacking her on the face and shoulders, fuming alcohol breath on the two of us in our one twin bed, raging that we were slobs, and I don't know how he knew to beat her instead of me because I don't remember there being any light on. We both cried in the dark, but then somehow we slept and in the morning when we woke the mother was frying up bacon, a baby slung over her shoulder, and the dad was happy and buoyant, thunderous in his praise of the pie now in the oven.

It was Sunday morning and I got to go to church with them. All the children got dressed up. The parents looked like movie stars, so handsome and young, carrying babies, shepherding the bigger kids, smooching in the car.

I loved every second of Catholic church. I loved the sickly sweet rotting-pomegranate smells of the incense. I loved the overwrought altar, the birdbath of holy water, the votive candles; I loved that there was a poor box, and the stations of the cross rendered in stained glass on the windows. I loved the curlicue angels in gold paint on the ceiling; I loved the woman selling holy cards. I loved the slutty older Catholic girls with their mean names, the ones with white lipstick and ratted hair that reeked of Aqua Net. I loved the drone of the priest intoning Latin. All that life surrounding you on all four sides *plus* the ceiling—it was like a religious bus station. They had all that stuff holding them together, and they got to be so conceited because they were *Catholics.*

Looking back on the God my friend believed in, he seems a little erratic, not entirely unlike her father—God as borderline personality. It was like believing in the guy who ran the dime store, someone with a kind face but who was always running behind and had already heard every one of your lame excuses a dozen times before—why you didn't have a receipt, why you hadn't noticed the product's flaw before you bought it. This God could be loving and reassuring one minute, sure that you had potential, and then fiercely disappointed the next, noticing every little mistake and just in general what a fraud you really were. He was a God whom his children could talk to, confide in, and trust, unless his mood shifted suddenly and he decided instead to blow up Sodom and Gomorrah.

My father's folks had been Presbyterian missionaries who raised their kids in Tokyo, and my father despised Christianity. He called Presbyterians "God's frozen people." My mother went to midnight mass on Christmas Eve at the Episcopal church in town, but no one in our family believed in God—it was like we'd all signed some sort of loyalty oath early on, agreeing not to believe in God in deference to the pain of my father's cold Christian childhood. I went to church with my grandparents sometimes and I loved it. It slaked my thirst. But I pretended to think it was foolish, because that pleased my father. I lived for him. He was my first god.

My mother and her twin sister had come over from Liverpool with their mother after their father died, when they were twelve. My mother had a lifelong compassion for immigrants; she used to find people waiting for boats to their homeland or waiting for money to be wired from the East so that they could catch a bus home, and she'd bring them to stay with us until everything was straightened out. She and my aunt Pat had been confirmed as Episcopalians in England—I have their confirmation picture on my mantel, two dark-haired beauties of twelve or so in long white baptismal-style dresses. But that was the last of their religious affiliation. My aunt Pat married a Jew, with a large Jewish family in tow, but they were not really Moses Jews; they were bagelly Jews. My closest cousin was bar mitzvahed, but other than accusing you of anti-Semitism if you refused second helpings of my uncle Millard's food, they might as well have been Canadians.

None of the adults in our circle believed. Believing meant that you were stupid. Ignorant people believed, uncouth people believed, and we were heavily couth. My dad was a writer, and my parents were intellectuals who went to the Newport Jazz festival every year for their vacation and listened to Monk and Mozart and the Modern Jazz Quartet. Everyone read all the time. Mt. Tamalpais loomed above us, and we hiked her windy trails many weekends, my dad with binoculars hanging around his neck because he was a serious bird-watcher. He worshiped in the church of Allen Ginsberg, at the Roger Tory Peterson Holiness Temple, the Tabernacle of Miles Davis.

We were raised to believe in books and music and nature. My mother played the piano most weekend nights, and all of us kids knew the words to almost every song in the *Fireside Book of Folk Songs*. When my parents' friends came over on the weekends and everyone had a lot to drink, my mother played piano and everyone sang: English ballads, spirituals, union songs, "The Golden Vanity," "Joe Hill," "Bread and Roses."

Their friends, our family friends, were like us; they read

as a vocation, worked for liberal causes, loved Dr. King and nature, smoked, drank a lot, liked jazz and gourmet food. They were fifties Cheever people, with their cocktails and affairs. They thought practicing Catholics insane, ridiculous in their beliefs, and morally wrong to have so many children; also, the non-Italian Catholics were terrible cooks. My mother made curries surrounded by ten kinds of condiments, including chutney she and her friends made every year in our kitchen. I bowed my head in bed and prayed, because I believed—not in Jesus—but in someone listening, someone who heard. I do not understand how that came to be; I just know I always believed and that I did not tell a soul. I did not tell a soul that strange boys rode by on bikes shouting racist insults about my kinky hair, or that we showed our naked bodies to the big boys in exchange for baseball cards, or that the Catholic dad had beat his daughter, because I wanted to be loved, and so I stood around silently, bursting with hope and secrets and fear, all skin and bone and eyes, with a crazy hair crown like that one ridiculous palm.

## Momcat

The Belvedere Lagoon was a body of green water surrounded on all sides by luxurious homes, each with a dock from which you might swim or launch a small Sunfish or rowboat. My best friend from second grade on was named Shelly. She was blonde, pretty, and had a sister one year younger, whose best friend was a girl named Pammy who lived at the other end of the lagoon.

Shelly's mother was a Christian Scientist. My father thought the Christian Scientists were so crazy that they actually made the Catholics look good. I was no longer close to the Catholics, as we had moved by this time into an old stone castle on Raccoon Straits on the north shore of San Francisco Bay. The castle had been built a hundred years before by a German man who wanted to make his new bride feel at home in California. It had trapdoors, a dungeon, and two caves in the back. My parents had bought it for twenty thousand dollars the year John Kennedy became president. My parents campaigned for him, my father looked like him, my mother quivered for him. She was like the preacher in *Cold Comfort Farm* whenever she talked about either of the Kennedys, trembling with indignant passion—"I'm *quivering* for you, Jack"—as if the rest of us didn't also love him.

We lived in this marvelous castle, but things were not going well inside its stone walls. My parents' marriage was not a very happy one, and everywhere you looked as the sixties traipsed along there was too much alcohol and pot and infidelity. But Shelly's parents did not drink at all, and their house was full of stability and warmth. Pammy and I were drawn to it like moths. Pammy's mother was an heiress and an alcoholic who weighed no more than eighty pounds and who had often passed out before breakfast. Her father was doing time in various California prisons for killing his mother's best friend.

So we came to this house on the lagoon where everyone looked so good and where the mother gathered her children (and any other loose kids who happened to be there) into an armchair, like Marmie in *Little Women,* and read to them from *Science and Health* or the Bible. She told you that you were a perfect child, that you were entirely good, and that everything was fine, all evidence to the contrary. She was kind, lovely, funny, an early feminist who wore huge Bermuda shorts and her husband's shirts and did not care what people thought of her. And she believed two of the most radical ideas I had ever heard: one, that God was both our Father *and* our Mother; and two, that I was beautiful. Not just in God's eyes, which didn't count—what's the point if Ed Sullivan was considered just as beautiful as Julie Christie? She meant physically, on the earth, a visibly pretty girl.

Now, I had skipped a grade, so I was a year younger than everyone else in my class, and at nine and ten and eleven was knee-knocking thin, with sharp wings for shoulder blades and wiry blonde hair that I wore short. All my life men had been nudging my dad and saying with great amusement that there must have been a nigger in the woodpile, I guess because of both the hair and my big heavy-lidded eyes. And my father, who never once in his life would have used the word *nigger,* would smile and give an almost imperceptible laugh—not a trace of rage on behalf of black people, not a trace of rage on behalf of me. I didn't even quite know what this phrase meant—I knew it meant that a black man must have been my father but I couldn't figure out how a woodpile figured in, since a woodpile housed only the most terrible things: snakes, spiders, rats, vermin, grub. The one time my older brother used the word *nigger,* he was grounded for a week. But when men whispered it to my father, he let it go. Why was this? Why would old lefties make this joke, and why would my dad act amused? Was it like spitting, a bad-boy thing? Did it make them feel tough for the moment, like rednecks for a day, so they could briefly sport grossness and muscles?

Lee, the Christian Science mother, smoothed my hair with her grandmother's boar-bristle brush, instead of tearing at it with a comb. She said that half the women in Belvedere would pay their beauticians anything for my hair's platinum color, and the roses in my cheeks, and the long skinny brown legs that carried me and her daughter into endless victories on the tennis courts.

Shelly was my first doubles partner. We were tennis champs.

It was so strange to be with families who prayed before the children left for school each day, before swim meets and work and tennis tournaments. Pammy would step over her mother on the way out the door and arrive at Shelly's house just as I did. At my house, no one had passed out on the floor, but my mom was scared and Dad was bored and my little brother was growing fat and my older brother was being called by the siren song of the counterculture. Pammy and I would walk in together and find Lee with her brood piled like puppies on top of her, in her armchair, reading the Bible. And she would pray for us all.

Shelly's house was the only place I could really sleep. At my own, I'd try to but would feel a threatening darkness hanging over the castle, as if my parents' bad marriage were casting shadows like giant wings—shadows of alcoholism, shadows of people at my parents' frequent parties who

necked in our rooms with people who were married to
somebody else. If I told my mom or dad, they said, Oh,
honey, *stop,* that's ridiculous, or they explained that everyone had had a lot to drink, as if what I'd seen didn't count
since it had sprung from a kind of accidental overdose. At
Christmas there were Fishhouse punches so alcoholic you
could have sterilized needles in them, and on hot summer
nights, blenders full of frappéed whiskey sours. The kids
were given sips or short glasses of drinks, and we helped
ourselves to more. By the age of twelve, all three of us were
drinking with some regularity. My mother did not drink
very much and so was frappé herself a lot; she was trying to
earn the money for law school, which was her dream, and
trying to get my dad to want to stay, and she looked tired,
scared, unhappy. But Pammy's mother made mine look
like Julie Andrews in *The Sound of Music.*

Many of the houses on the lagoon held children who by
thirteen were drinking and using pot, LSD, cocaine, and
heroin. Five children I knew well from school or the tennis
courts died in the sixties—three of overdose, one by hanging, and the boy who lived directly across the lagoon
drowned in its cool waters.

I remember how disgusted my parents were whenever
they heard that Lee had taken her kids in to see a practi-
tioner, instead of an M.D., when they got sick, as if she had
entrusted her kids to a leech specialist. They were hardly
ever sick, though. I don't think they even got poison oak. I
was sick much more often than Shelly was. My mother was
always basting at least one of us kids with calamine lotion. I
remember being sick with chest colds and croup, sitting on

my mother's lap on the toilet seat while scalding water from the shower filled the room with steam, characters in a hot, misty fairy tale, breathing together till I was better.

Pammy and I basked in Lee's love like lizards on sunny rocks. Lee lay beside me in bed when I couldn't sleep and whispered the Twenty-third Psalm to me: "'The Lord is my shepherd, I shall not want'—I am not wanting for *any*-thing, Annie. Let's find a green pasture inside us to rest in. Let's find the still waters within." She'd lay beside me quietly for a while as we listened to the tide of the lagoon lap against the dock. Then she'd go on: "'Yea, though I walk *through* the valley of the shadow of death,' Annie, not 'Yea, as I end up living forever in the valley. . . .'" And she prayed for the Good Shepherd to gather my thoughts like sheep. I did not quite believe in the power of her Mother-Father God, because my frightened lamby thoughts seemed to be stampeding toward a wall, piling up on each other's backs, bleating plaintively while their wild eyes darted around frantically. But I believed in Lee, and I felt her arms around me. I could hear Shelly's even breathing in the next bed, sense Lee's younger daughter and Pammy asleep in the next room, and the whole house would be so quiet, no shadows at all, and Lee would whisper me to sleep.

## B-plus

I was on tennis courts all over California the year we invaded Cambodia, the year Janis Joplin and Jimi Hendrix died, the year the students were killed at Kent State. I was at tournaments up and down the state with my doubles partner Bee. I was sixteen, a little bit fat in the can by now. Her mother Mimi drove us around the state in an old Country Squire station wagon. My own mother didn't know how to drive, and besides, she was putting herself through law school. We hardly saw her.

Mimi had prematurely white hair and a huge smile, sang songs from musicals as she drove along, and always reminded me of Carol Channing. She used to say that I was the most "utterly marvelous girl." Bee and I had been ranked number one in the state the year before in sixteen-and-under doubles, but my game was beginning to fall apart. In singles, Bee was thriving, but I was no longer in the top ten and that was very painful. I had two lives now, one with Bee on the green hardcourts and occasional grass, and one with Pammy, with whom I now went to school. We attended a little hippie high school in San Francisco and were two of the best students. There were fifty kids in my graduating class, many of them troubled children from San Francisco's socialite families. It was 1970 and we were smoking a lot of dope, which we could buy upstairs on the second floor of the schoolhouse in the student lounge. Two kids overdosed on heroin that year, although only one died, and a sweet rich boy of fifteen, on LSD, ran into the surf at Ocean Beach and was never seen again. We could buy balls of hashish soaked in opium for five dollars each. Pammy and I were getting drunk whenever possible, and then I was showing up for tennis matches hungover and really uninterested, except that I loved Bee and Mimi so much and had spent the last four years practically living at their house. They were wealthy, and Mimi had exquisite taste. I rarely saw the Christian Scientists anymore, though Pammy was still close to them. We all went to different schools, and I did not live near them on the lagoon, as Pammy did, so although I still loved them, I was with Bee and Mimi now. Mimi was an artist, a painter, who claimed me as daughter number two. She and Bee fought; she and I didn't. Bee and I wore our hair in pigtails, tied in bright ribbons. Bee had brown hair, brown eyes, brown limbs, freckles.

Pammy looked like a Renaissance angel in tie-dye, with white-blonde electric hair the color of Maryiln Monroe's, angel hair like you put on Christmas trees, and her skin was as fair as a baby's. Her breasts were large, and she was always a little overweight; she refused for political reasons to be thin. We were high on the women's movement; the voices from New York were like foghorns saving us in the night, but they also frightened us because they were so strident. I spent the night at Pammy's a lot; there we could swim in the lagoon, or sunbathe on the dock, and get away with almost anything, day or night. So Pammy and I sailed and swam and smoked dope and drank "spoolie-oolies," which were glasses of red wine and 7UP. We listened to Stephane Grapelli, because Pammy played flute, and we listened to Scott Joplin before anyone else, because she also played classical piano. She took lessons from an old blind Russian named Lev Shore, who was the father she should have had. Her father was still in prison. She was a little in love with my father, who was so much hipper than most of the other dads. He still lived with my mother, although things had continued to deteriorate around our house. But he took Pammy, my younger brother, and me to the beach on weekends, and his friends smoked dope with us and served us jug red wine.

I wasn't thinking about God that much, except that when I was stoned I felt a mystical sense of peace and expansion, and I secretly thought I might become a Buddhist one of these days. There were many Buddhists my father admired—Gary Snyder, Peter Matthiessen, Alan Watts. My father by then was practicing transcendental meditation, which he'd first investigated for a book he wrote while Ronald Reagan was governor, called *Anti-California: Report from Our First Para-Fascist State.*

At any rate, Pammy and I had an English teacher our sophomore year whom we loved, a large long-haired woman named Sue who wore purple almost exclusively and was a friendly hippie sort. She was one of the best teachers I've ever had. Her hair fell to her chair like a puppet-show curtain. She made you want to be a teacher, to throw the lights on for children that way.

After school Pammy and I would drive home in her mother's car or hitchhike if we'd ridden in on the ferry, and then she would go off to her music lessons, and I would go to practice with Bee at the courts by the deserted railroad tracks.

Pammy and I did really well in school, mostly A's and A-minuses, a few B-pluses. At Pammy's house, she and her three sisters forged their mother Mary's signature to their report cards, since Mary was such a mess she did not seem to be aware that report cards needed to be signed or, for that matter, were even given out. In a way life was easier there than over at my house, because at least it was consistent: Mary was *always* a drunken mess, Pammy's father was always in prison. Over at my house, things could go any number of ways. I have read since that this is how you induce psychosis in rats: you behave inconsistently with them; you keep changing the rules. One day when they press down the right lever, expecting a serving of grain like they've always gotten before, they instead get a shock. And eventually the switching back and forth drives them mad, while the rats who get shocked every time they press the lever figure it out right away and work around it. Pammy worked around it. She had other mothers, like I did, and inside herself she grew the mother she had needed all those years.

So I was doing well academically, and I was a well-ranked tennis player and was the apple of my handsome father's eye—and then I would bring home a report card with a B-plus on it, and my parents would look at the report card as if I'd flunked. "Uh, honey?" one of them would ask, looking perplexed. "Now, this isn't a criticism but, if you could get a B-plus in philosophy, how much harder would it have been to get an A-minus?"

It never once occurred to me to stare back at them and say, "What a *crock*." I just felt shame that I had disappointed them again, and I felt that if I could do a little better, Mom and Dad would get along again, my big brother would come home more often, and neither my mom nor my brother Steve would be fat. Stevo was the only person in the family who loved and was loved by every other member of the family, but—or so—he was the sacrificial lamb, hiding politely upstairs in his room, watching our small TV, tending to his baseball-card collection. If I could just do a little better, I would finally have the things I longed for—a sense of OKness and connection and meaning and peace of mind, a sense that my family was OK and that we were good people. I would finally know that we were safe, and that my daddy wasn't going to leave us, and that I would be loved someday.

Drugs helped. More than anything else, they gave me the feeling that I was fine and life was good and something sacred shimmered at its edges.

Being sexual with boys helped, too. Being sexual with anybody helped—there was a girl named Deborah at our school, a full-tilt hippie who wore her long blonde hair up and antique lace blouses over Indian-print skirts and who looked like Liv Ullman. She used to hold a Lifesaver between her teeth and have me close mine around the half that was showing so that our lips, our open mouths, met as I'd take the Lifesaver into my own mouth, and I would feel my insides grow hard and quivery. Being loved by my teachers helped, but then report cards would come out, and once again I would think I had fallen short.

I was thirty-five when I discovered that a B-plus was a really good grade.

I played tennis all that summer of 1970, sometimes hungover, always finding the kids at the tournament dances who had the beer or the Boone Farm strawberry wine, and I drank with them while Bee went to bed early. Someone would find me half passed out with boys on boats, or barfing in the girls' room, or smoking a joint in someone's car, and I would be delivered home. Once I played a finals match with a huge blister on my top lip, the kind nursing babies get, only I got mine from trying to get one more hit off a roach the size of a grain of rice. When I was with Pammy, between tournaments, tanning on the dock of her house, slathered in baby oil, listening to her mother rant around inside, I felt like I could breathe. When I spent the night there, we'd stay up watching Dick Cavett with her older sister, and her mother would wake up long enough to come into the TV room and screech, "I hate you fucking goddamn shitfuck Lamotts, and your father's Commie bullshit," and we'd all say, "Hi, Mary," or "Hi, Mom," and she'd say, "OK, well, good night, girls, good night, Annie," and we'd all say liltingly, "Good niiiiight," without taking our eyes off the screen.

When I stayed at Bee's house, we went to bed early, giggled all night in the dark, then got up early, ate protein for breakfast, and headed to the courts.

When Pammy and I returned to school in the fall of my junior year, terrible news unfolded: our English teacher Sue had become a born-again Christian. And apparently all the students who were her friends, about a dozen or so, had been brought into the fold during the later summer, and now they all met in the courtyard during lunch to pray, to read from the Bible, and to beam at each other with amusement. Sue would still hand out the most wonderful poems in her class—Sylvia Plath and Auden, T. S. Eliot, Ferlinghetti—but now she interpreted everything in Christian terms; it was all viewed through Christ's eyes and determined to be about resurrection or original sin. Ferlinghetti writing "I am waiting for the rebirth of wonder" opened the way for a short talk on the hunger of the unsaved person; Sylvia Plath's "Daddy" was about her father, of course, but it also referred to Jehovah. I wept in Sue's class at the betrayal, and at her gentle patronizing efforts to console me.

Then Pammy and I fought back. We read the great atheists, studied their reasoning, especially Bertrand Russell's essay "Why I Am Not a Christian," which we basically memorized. We challenged Sue on everything, every assertion, even when she was right. When we studied the Dylan song "Dear Landlord," I valiantly tried to convince the class that Dylan was actually peeved with the earthly and unjust owner of the house that he was renting. Sue and the saved students listened with great gentleness and then looked tenderly around the room at one another.

I realized for the first time in my life that I was capable of murder.

I told my father that night, and he was deeply sympathetic, since no one disliked Christians more than he. He offered me a glass of wine with dinner. My mother was in the city studying for a law school exam. My dad and I ended up getting drunk together for the first time. Emboldened by the wine, I asked him how he'd feel if I quit competitive tennis. He'd never been that keen on it to begin with, as he was not at all athletic, and he said I should do whatever my heart told me. When I went to bed that night, I knew my tennis days were over, and when I finished my last year as Bee's doubles partner in the girls sixteen and under, I gave my racket to the Goodwill, and I never got another migraine again.

### Candle Salad

There were endless lawns, fields, and meadows on the grounds of the small women's college I attended in the East. I had already announced my plans to drop out at the end of my sophomore year to become a writer, so I just took English and philosophy; I didn't have to fulfill any of the requirements necessary to graduate. I was on the tennis team and played junior varsity basketball; I also took religion, in deference to this puzzling thing inside me that had begun to tug on my sleeve from time to time, trying to get my attention. I've read that Augustine said that to look for God is to find him, but I was not looking for God, not really. Or at any rate I didn't know I was.

I also started getting laid with some regularity. I was spearheading the campus McGovern movement and in love with a man who was running the entire Baltimore campaign. It was not at all convenient to fit classes and homework into this schedule.

I smoked a lot of dope that year and sat beneath the trees. There was a huge silver maple near my dormitory with big palmate leaves. In March you could look up through the branches and see puzzle pieces of blue sky. Then day by day the bright green leaves opened like fingers, until the canopy had filled in, like carpet in the sky.

I don't think I ever said the word *Jew* until college, although our house and town and tennis clubs had been filled with Jewish people—that's what we called them:

"Jewish people." I believed you weren't supposed to call them Jews unless you were one. My aunt Pat's husband and kids were secular Jews, so I suppose they *could* have called themselves "Jews," but I don't think they did. Neither did my parents' Jewish friends. They just *were* Jewish, maybe a little more so than they were also Type AB or O positive, but not much more. In college, though, most of the smartest, funniest women in our dorm, the ones who always had the best dope, were Jews and referred endlessly to their Jewishness. It was exhilarating, and I wanted to be one of them. I'd thought for a while, and especially since Pammy and I had become strident atheists, that Jews were better, smarter, hipper than the rest of us. If you were Jewish, you were part of the tribe that included Lenny Bruce and Bette Midler. Allen Ginsberg was one of you, and Mel Brooks, and Woody Allen. The women we revered were Jews: Grace Paley, Hannah Arendt, Bella Abzug, Gloria Steinem. Ram Dass, who'd started out at Harvard as Richard Alpert but had just come back from India a Hindu convert, called himself a Hin-Jew. Most of the girls I wanted to be like were Jews, and in comparison, the rest of us looked like we'd come from Grand Rapids.

One of my friends in college took me home to visit her mother one three-day weekend. Her mother Billie was big and fat and unbelievably beautiful, except that she sported a heavy beard—a real beard, like three-day stubble. She acted like she'd known me forever. When I woke up in her house that first morning, she had shaved for the occasion and put pancake makeup over the stubble. It looked like she had a thousand blackheads.

She was a Zionist and convinced me that Israel should bomb the shit out of Syria, and by the time I'd finished my grapefruit, I too believed this to be obvious. I asked her if she went to temple, and she acted as if I'd asked if she frequently used an escort service.

"Of *course* not," she said. "What's there for me? You sit, they don't speak English, only the men count for much, you wait forever for a song you might understand, you check out what everyone is wearing? And what's the pitch—you're born, you die, you go into a box? What's so tempting there?"

"But, Mom," cried my friend, "you *never* let us go out on Friday nights."

"You should be out gallivanting on the Sabbath?"

All my life people thought I looked Jewish—or rather, the ones who didn't think I was mulatto thought I might be a Jew. And when my friends in college said that I *felt* like a Jew to them, I understood this to be a great compliment.

They always threw their arms around me and hugged me while crying out Yiddish endearments. Yet none of them believed in God. They believed in social justice, good works, Israel, and Bette Midler. I was nearly thirty before I met a religious Jew. All these girls had been bat mitzvahed, but when I asked why they weren't religious, they shrugged. "Maybe," they said, "it's hard to believe in a God who would not stop the Holocaust."

I had established a bar in my dorm room with my roommate Amy, who was not a Jew or a believer. It was called the Roly-Poly Bar and Grill, because we had both gained so much weight our freshman years. It was open every weekend night, and there were always a number of friends who, like Amy, played great blues guitar and sang and knew all the words to those early Bonnie Raitt albums and drank and smoked dope and sometimes took the Dexedrine the infirmary passed out. We talked all night. Everything felt so intense and coiled and Möbius strip–like, all those drinks and drugs and hormones making everything constantly double back over itself. There were lots of girls in love with lots of other girls, and all of us half in love with the lesbian radical wing of the faculty, because they were giving us our lives, giving us back the lives our mothers had lost, but I was seeing the McGovern man while in love with another man back home, and I felt like I'd always felt: the stranger in a strange land. I was desperately homesick for my father and younger brother and Pammy. The times I felt most functional were when I was drinking at the Roly-Poly Bar and Grill or smoking pot under a tree with my friends.

The smell of the eastern spring was so different from spring in California. Maybe it was the lack of marine smells, the salt, the algae. Maybe because everything was so cold and barren in the winter, the smell of spring greenness was much more acute. And there were so many different kinds of birds—mockingbirds, chickadee-dee-dees, and crows as big as cats. But the most amazing thing of all were the redbud trees. They would bud at the end of winter: in all that twiggy stick world of gray, buds bloomed pinker than cherry blossoms, Renoir-cheek pink.

I read Thomas Merton, Simone Weil, William Blake,

Rumi. I was thirsty for something that I will dare to call the truth, so I read a lot of East Indian poetry and sat in the little chapel on campus and tried to pray. In the spring of my sophomore year, I began a course with a tiny Czechoslovakian woman named Eva Gossman. I loved Mrs. Gossman in general and worked very hard in her class. Then one day she gave us Kierkegaard's *Fear and Trembling,* and my life changed forever.

Eva Gossman loved Kierkegaard in the same way she loved Chekhov, and she took us through *Fear and Trembling* slowly. We read a lot of it out loud in class. Kierkegaard retold the story of Abraham, who heard God's angels tell him to take his darling boy Isaac up to the mountain and offer him as a sacrifice. Now, this was exactly the sort of Old Testament behavior I had trouble with. It made me think that this God was about as kind and stable as Judge Julius Hoffman of Chicago Seven fame. But the way Kierkegaard wrote it, Abraham understood that all he really had in life was God's unimaginable goodness and love, God's promise of protection, God's paradoxical promise that Isaac would provide him with many descendants. He understood that without God's love and company, this life would be so empty and barbaric that it almost wouldn't matter whether his son was alive or not. And since this side of the grave you could never know for sure if there was a God, you had to make a leap of faith, if you could, leaping across the abyss of doubt with fear and trembling.

So Abraham walked to the mountaintop with his son. Isaac asked his father where they were going, and Abraham answered that they were going to the mountain to sacrifice a lamb, and Isaac, who was small but nobody's fool, said, Well, then, uh—where's that rascally lamb? Abraham answered that God would provide the lamb. They walked together up the mountain, Abraham grievous but trusting in his God. When they arrived, Abraham got his knife but *finally* an angel called to him from Heaven and told him that he had successfully shown his devotion to God. And the Lord had indeed provided a lamb, which was trapped in a thicket nearby.

In the interior silence that followed my understanding of this scene, I held my breath for as long as I could, sitting there under the fluorescent lights—and then I crossed over. I don't know how else to put it or how and why I actively made, if not exactly a *leap* of faith, a lurch of faith. It was like Jacques Tati—Mr. Hulot—making his way across a rickety ladder that spanned a crevasse. I left class believing—accepting—that there was a God. I did not understand how this could have happened. It made no sense. It made no sense that what brought me to this conviction was the story of a God who would ask his beloved Abraham to sacrifice the child he loved more than life itself. It made no sense that Abraham could head for the mountain in Moriah still believing in God's goodness. It made no sense that even as he walked his son to the sacrificial altar, he still believed God's promise that Isaac would give him many descendants. It made no sense that he was willing to do the one thing in the world he could not do, just because God told him to. God told him to obey and to believe that he was a loving god and could be trusted. So Abraham did obey.

I felt changed, and a little crazy. But though I was still like a stained and slightly buckled jigsaw puzzle with some pieces missing, now there were at least a few border pieces in place.

One day I told my friends. And my closest Jewish friend clapped her hands to her cheeks, as if she were a mother just told that her daughter had begun menstruating, and then she went to tell the others.

She and her friends determined that I must be bat mitzvahed.

They also decided, as one, that even though I was not actually becoming a Jew, I must learn to speak phonetic Hebrew, so I was assigned a tutor. *Baruch atah Adonai Eloheinu* . . . I was trained in Yiddish: I'm plotzing! Oy, I'm plotzing a bissle. I was given my Hebrew name, Simcha, which means joy. I was drilled on Jewish culture and practice:

"Do Jews camp?" I was asked by the woman who would play the rabbi in the service, scheduled for a month hence in one of the dorm's recreation rooms.

"Yes?" I guessed.

"No! Jews don't camp! That's very important."

Later, stoned, under a tree, I asked her, *"Why?"*

"Outside there are soldiers, and wolves. You should be at home with what's comfortable, all your communications needs at hand. *Believe* me, you don't want to be outside, because anything could happen. And remember: anything did happen."

"Why are Jews so smart?"

"Survival of the fittest. Always on the run, living by our

wits, not allowed the trappings of land, not allowed to get fat and dumb—it made us smart and fierce."

"Does your mother believe in God?"

"My mother believes in steak and fur. My father believes in hard work."

"Won't we need a prayer for the service?"

"Yes, of *course* yes. And Simcha, as your rabbi, I've gone ahead and selected the prayer. This is a prayer my mother's friend Kim composed, which she said every night at bedtime. Maybe most of us aren't religious anymore, but we are an ethical people:

> *Help for the sick and hungry,*
> *home for the homeless folk,*
> *peace in the world forever,*
> *this is my prayer, O Lord. Amen.*

I was taught some Hebrew scripture. I was told to memorize a recipe for Candle Salad, which was in a book called *The Jewish Home Beautiful*: on a leaf of lettuce, you put a ring of canned pineapple. Into its center, insert half a banana, vertically. Secure part of an orange slice with a toothpick to the ring of pineapple, so the banana shouldn't topple over, God forbid; and on top, for the flame, a maraschino cherry.

We had the service the night before spring vacation began. It was a strangely warm night, the air perfumed with trees in blossom. I had found the perfect dress in a secondhand store—a light blue eyelet empire—and someone had made a wreath of flowers for my hair. The room we'd reserved was filled with candles and flowers, incense, and this being a Reform event, a platter of Bob Ostrow cold cuts. One of the seniors had bought several bottles of Manischweitz blackberry wine, which turned out to be like something you could pour over pancakes. There were a dozen friends in tow, besides the people in the service. The cantor sang beautiful Hebrew holy songs. The rabbi, with a long gray beard and a yarmulke, cleared her throat to begin. My roommate Amy was my mother, with powdered Gibson-girl hair and a padded bosom. Two friends were dressed up as my weepy aunts from Florida. One tall friend was my father, another the grandpa who kept clapping her hands over her ears and saying, "Mein leetle Simcha."

The service began: the rabbi had me recite my Hebrew, my mother wept, the aunts tried to console her, and that was so lovely; none of us were shaving our legs or armpits anymore, so my mother and aunts were hirsute as Esau. "I am a *hairy* auntie," one of them kept proclaiming. I recited part of Psalm Ninety-one, which says, "He shall cover you with his feathers, and under his wings you shall take refuge." The rabbi asked me a number of questions to establish that I had studied for this day, but the only one I remember was "Do we like to camp?"

Then I said tearfully how happy I was to have such friends, to have become a woman this day, who knew what she wanted to be, and we ended with the words of the prophet Micah: "And what does the Lord require of you, but to do justice, and to love mercy, and to walk humbly with your God."

*Lichen*

In August of 1977, Duxberry Reef was green with the crust called lichen, made of algae and fungus; it covered the lava rock like slippery fabric. Lichen is what reduces rock to soil and sand. It was a heathery, sage green.

I was twenty-three, out of school four years, writing and cleaning houses and teaching tennis. I still believed in God, although I did not talk about it with my father much. He didn't mind my recounting adventures on LSD, or romantic dramas even if they involved married men, but the God business made him act impatient with me. So I had gone underground with it again. That day we were walking along on the lava beds, peering down into the tide pools— my father, who was fifty-four, and my brother Steve, who we still called Stevo. He was eighteen. My brother John lived on the other side of the mountain with his girlfriend and came over once a week. Our mother was a lawyer in Honolulu by then. We had a black lab named Muldoon.

If my father worshiped anything it was the beauty of nature. The tide pools were full of wafting hairlike algae and wonderful kelp like emerald green lasagna noodles. You had to be very careful when bending down to inspect the creatures who lived in the pools, or you'd fall on your butt. Spiky sea urchins dug in the crevices of the lava rocks; sea anemones, highly pigmented in August, yellow, pink, deep red; lots of little crabs picking their way through the algae and kelp. The three of us were paying even more attention than usual, trying to tether ourselves to the earth, because the world was coming to an end.

My dad had fallen over a week before while walking along Shattuck Avenue near the Berkeley campus. He had been there to do some research at the university. He wasn't hurt when he toppled over. Someone helped him up and he dusted himself off with good-natured embarrassment, but he did mention it at dinner that night at his girlfriend's house, and also that he'd been feeling strange lately, like his head didn't quite work. He was trim and in wonderful health, in love, with all of his children nearby. We all promised it would turn out to be nothing.

But it was going to be something, and I think I knew that. He had confided in me that working had been very perplexing lately: he'd start to type one thought down, and something altogether different would come out. It was like the computer inside his head was not communicating with the printer.

Still, he looked good, tall and fair, thick brown hair flecked with gray, blue-gray eyes and a long beaky nose that somehow worked on him. He wore and had always worn chinos, or jeans, and moccasins, field binoculars around his neck. That day at Duxberry, pelicans flew by so low to the water you'd think their bellies were wet with surf, and there were hundreds of seagulls, cormorants, Arctic terns, geese and ducks and egrets and herons.

I could remember being here at three on my father's shoulders as he walked along with my mother below the cliffs. Stevo hadn't been born yet, and my brother John ran up ahead, always wanting to distance himself from the rest of us. When I was eight and nine, with Stevo by then toddling along, we collected agate-sized pieces of fossilized whalebone: hard dark rocks with chambers like the eyes of a bee. We gathered them into the tiny muslin bags with yellow drawstrings that fishing weights came in. My father paid us a quarter for collecting all the whalebone we could find, and it kept us busy and attentive, on our hands and knees, pawing slowly through the agates and pebbles and sand.

Now my father, brother, and I were all living in Bolinas, my father with his girlfriend and Steve. I was in our one-room cabin. All of us were drinking a lot with much pleasure.

There were marvelous islands of green in the water that day, kelp forests swaying with the water currents as if to a symphony. My father was very distracted, deep in thought, looking up from time to time. Stevo and I were focused on the tide pools, outwardly calm and engaged but secretly panicking, huddling together whenever Dad went off to study something new. We were waiting for the results of a CAT scan that Dad had taken a few days before. There might even be a message on his answering machine when we got back from our walk.

Steve slipped on the wet lava; it was slick and rich with marine vegetation—walking there was like stepping around on someone's wet head. He fell on his bottom and began to berate himself, close to tears. He was a senior in high school, no longer fat. Now he was too tall, too gangly, very dependent on Dad and me. He had gone to live in Hawaii with Mom when she'd first moved there a few years before, but he'd been beaten up by a native at a bus stop and had moved back to Bolinas not long after. He sat on the rock and didn't get up, his hand was in a fist like he might hit someone, and then instead he began to hit the palm of his other hand, the way you work a baseball mitt.

My dad looked away from Stevo to give him a chance to collect himself. He pointed to where a hawk hung just above the wall of cliffs which runs the length of the beach. There are often tiny avalanches in process here, pebbles and dirt clods tumbling down the cliffs' sheer faces. Nature had never let my father down and never would. He often repeated the old saying that Nature bats last. I on the other hand was totally doubtful about whether God was going to be of any help at all if I lost my father.

"Come on, buddy, you're OK. Get up," my father said kindly, reaching out a hand. My brother didn't take it for a minute. He was wild with anxiety. He was very young to have to go through what was unfolding that day as our family's destiny. We were, in fact, going to learn later that afternoon that my father had a brain tumor on the word section of his brain, a metastasized melanoma, something no one had ever survived at that time. In just a week or so, doctors were going to take out as much of the tumor as they could, but they weren't going to be able to get it all; its tentacles reached deep inside his brain. He was going to come home from the hospital to his girlfriend's house looking like Dr. Frankenstein had had a go at him. He was going to have the most aggressive forms of radiation and chemotherapy available, be part of a clinical trial that wouldn't work for him; he was going to have one good year in between these treatments where he would be able to work off and on, and walk with us every day; he was going to live to see John graduate from Berkeley; he was going to live to see my younger brother graduate from high school; he was going to live to see me sell a novel about our family to a fancy New York publisher; he was going to live to read a draft of it while his brain was still functioning. But then the cancer was going to start to eat away at his mind, and he was slowly going to end up like a huge friendly toddler. He was going to have to bear knowing for a while that his mind was going; he was going to have to bear letting his kids and girlfriend dress him, clean him, feed him; he was going to end up living at the one-room cabin with me and Steve, his girlfriend and oldest friends around, playing Pete Seeger on the stereo, and Billie Holliday, Joan Baez, and Mozart, the Modern Jazz Quartet. He was going to end up in a coma a month before he died, the cabin turned into a hospice room and us the stricken nurses. My father's handsome fair face was going to have tumors on it— *tumors* on the skin that today was flushed with health. The cancer was going to spread like a chain of stores, and he was going to need morphine and catheters and lemon swabs and fleecy bedding. Maybe he would hear the music we played on the stereo in the cabin, maybe he would be aware of us watching him through the night, but what we did not know that day on the lava rock was that he was going to die two years from this August morning—this morning when the three of us were walking about peering into tide pools, with our dog Muldoon bumping into our legs, the late-summer diffusion of light making everything in the pools seem larger: the sea anemones, the bloom of algae, the tiny crabs.


## Cracks

From the hills of Tiburon, Belvedere Island looks like a great green turtle with all of its parts pulled in. It's covered with eucalyptus, cedars, rhododendrons, manicured lawns.

I had come back to live in Tiburon. It was 1982, I was twenty-eight, and I had just broken up with a man in a neighboring county. He was the love of my life, and I of his, but things were a mess. We were taking a lot of cocaine and psychedelic mushrooms, and drinking way too much. When I moved out, he moved back in with his wife and son. My dad had been dead for three years. My mother still practiced law in Hawaii, my oldest brother John had moved even farther away, and my younger brother had, in the most incongruous act of our family's history, joined the army.

When my boyfriend and I split up, I had called a divorced friend named Pat who'd lived in Tiburon for twenty years; I had baby-sat for her kids when I was young. She had loved me since I was eleven. I said I needed a place to regroup for a couple of weeks. Then I stayed for a year and a half. (Let this be a lesson.)

She worked in the city all day so I had the house to myself. I woke up quite late every morning, always hungover, the shades drawn, the air reeking of cigarettes and booze. The whole time I stayed at her house, I kept drinking from her one bottle of Dewars. Most nights I'd sip wine or beer while she and I hung out, eating diet dinners together. Then after she'd gone to bed nice and early every night, I'd pour myself the first of sixteen ounces of Scotch. I'd put music on the stereo—Bruce Springsteen, Tom Petty—and dance. Sometimes I would dance around with a drink in my hand. Other times, I would toss down my drink and then sit on the couch in reveries—of romance, of seeing my dad again, of being on TV talk shows, chatting with Johnny Carson, ducking my head down while the audience laughed at my wit, then reaching demurely for my glass of Scotch. My self-esteem soared, and when the talk show ended in my mind, I would dance.

I took a sleeping pill with the last glass of Scotch every night, woke up late, wrote for a couple of hours, and then walked to one of four local liquor stores to buy a pint of Dewars. Back at Pat's, I would pour the whiskey back into the big bottle, raising the level back to where it had been before I started the night before. Then I'd put the empty in a brown paper bag and take off for the bike path to dispose of it.

There were many benches along the way with beautiful views of Richardson Bay. Some of them had trash cans next to them, but others did not, and I'd be frantic to get rid of my empty bottles. Certainly someone might interpret them as a sign that I had developed some sort of drinking problem. But sometimes I'd be forced to leave the bag on a bench where there was no trash can, and I lived in terror of someone running up to me holding out the paper bag, calling, "Oh, Misssss, you forgot something." Then they'd drop it, and it would shatter inside the brown bag, and the jig would be up.

I was scared much of the time. There were wonderful aspects to my life—I was writing, I loved my friends, I lived amidst all this beauty. I got to walk with Pammy several times a week, along the bike path or over in Mill Valley where she was living happily ever after with her husband. Every night I'd swear I wouldn't hit Pat's Scotch again, maybe instead just have a glass of wine or two. But then she'd go to bed, and without exactly meaning to, I'd find myself in the kitchen, quietly pouring a drink.

Life was utterly schizophrenic. I was loved and often seemed cheerful, but fear pulsed inside me. I was broke, clearly a drunk, and also bulimic. One night I went to bed so drunk and stuffed with food that I blacked out. When I awoke, feeling quite light, I got on the scale. Then I called Pat at work with my great news: "I lost five pounds last night!"

"And I found it," she said. It seemed she had cleaned up after me.

I made seven thousand dollars that year and could not afford therapy or enough cocaine. Then my married man called again, and we took to meeting in X-rated motels with lots of coke, tasteful erotic romps on TV like *The Bitch of the Gestapo*. But it was hard for him to get away. I'd pine away at Pat's, waiting for her to go to sleep so I could dance.

I was cracking up. It was like a cartoon where something gets hit, and one crack appears, which spiderwebs outward until the whole pane or vase is cracked and hangs suspended for a moment before falling into a pile of powder on the floor. I had not yet heard the Leonard Cohen song in which he sings, "There are cracks, cracks, in everything, that's how the light gets in." I had the cracks but not the hope.

In pictures of Pammy and me taken then, she weighs a lot more than I. I'm skinny, insubstantial, as if I want to disappear altogether and my body is already starting to, piece by piece like the Cheshire cat. Pammy looks expansive and buttery and smiling. I look furtive, like a deer surprised in a heinous act.

I'm always squinting in these pictures, too, baffled, suspicious—get this over with, my eyes say. Pammy's hair is no longer wild blonde hippie-girl hair. Now it falls in soft waves to her shoulders. My hair is in a long fuzzy Afro, a thicket behind which I'm trying to hide. Pammy gives off natural charm, like someone who is dangling a line with something lovely attached, saying, Come play with us— we're worth it! While I'm saying, Go away! Stop bothering me!

I kept the extent of my drinking a secret from her. And in a show of control, played to an often empty house, I'd try to wait until five for the first beer. But this other person inside me would start crying, Help me. So I'd get us a little something to tide us over.

It was so frustrating to be in love with an unavailable married man that of course I found a second one. He was a dentist, who met me in fancy hotels, with lots of cocaine and always some Percodan to take the edge off. He was also doing nitrous oxide after hours, but he wouldn't share. I tried everything to get him to bring me a little soupçon of nitrous, but never got it. When he reported one night that his wife had torn at one of her eyes in despair over our affair and that he'd taken her to Emergency four days before, I thought, *God,* is your wife a mess."

But a feather of truth floated inside the door of my mind that night—the truth that I was crossing over to the dark side. I still prayed but was no longer sure anyone heard. I called a suicide hot line two days later, but hung up when someone answered. Heaven forbid someone should think I needed help. I was a Lamott—Lamotts *give* help.

I kept walking into town on the bike path to dispose of my bottle and buy another; the path was where the railroad tracks used to be. I'd turn right on Beach Road and walk along the west shore of Belvedere Island, passing below the big concrete Episcopal church on the hill. I'd actually spent some time at St. Stephen's as a child. My mother and I would go there for Midnight Mass on Christmas Eve every year, and I went with assorted friends every so often. It looked like a PG&E substation. I'd heard from family friends that there was a new guy preaching, named Bill Rankin, an old civil rights priest who had gotten this stolid congregation mobilized behind issues of peace and justice. I wasn't remotely ready for Christianity, though—I mean, I wasn't *that* far gone.

Still, I had never stopped believing in God since that day in Eva Gossman's class. Mine was a patchwork God, sewn together from bits of rag and ribbon, Eastern and Western, pagan and Hebrew, everything but the kitchen sink and Jesus.

Then one afternoon in my dark bedroom, the cracks webbed all the way through me. I believed that I would die soon, from a fall or an overdose. I knew there was an afterlife but felt that the odds of my living long enough to get into heaven were almost nil. They couldn't possibly take you in the shape I was in. I could no longer imagine how God could love me.

But in my dark bedroom at Pat's that afternoon, out of nowhere it crossed my mind to call the new guy at St. Stephen's.

So I did. He was there, and I started to explain that I was losing my mind, but he interrupted to say with real anguish that he was sorry but he had to leave. He literally begged me to call back in the morning, but I couldn't form any words in reply. It was like in the movies when the gangster is blowing bubbles through the bullet hole in his neck. There was this profound silence, except for my bubbling. Then he said, "Listen. Never mind. I'll wait. Come on in."

It took me forty-five minutes to walk there, but this skinny middle-aged guy was still in his office when I arrived. My first impression was that he was smart and profoundly tenderhearted. My next was that he was really listening, that he could hear what I was saying, and so I let it all tumble out—the X-rated motels, my father's death, a hint that maybe every so often I drank too much.

I don't remember much of his response, except that when I said I didn't think God could love me, he said, "God *has* to love you. That's God's job." Some years later I asked him to tell me about this first meeting. "I felt," he said, "that you had gotten yourself so tangled up in big God questions that it was suffocating you. Here you were in a rather desperate situation, suicidal, clearly alcoholic, going down the tubes. I thought the trick was to help you extricate yourself enough so you could breathe again. You said your prayers weren't working anymore, and I could see that in your desperation you were trying to save *yourself*: so I said you should stop praying for a while, and let me pray for you. And right away, you seemed to settle down inside."

"What did you hear in my voice when I called?"

"I just heard that you were in trouble."

He was about the first Christian I ever met whom I could stand to be in the same room with. Most Christians seemed almost hostile in their belief that they were saved and you weren't. Bill said it bothered him too, but you had to listen to what was underneath their words. What did it mean to be saved, I asked, although I knew the word smacked of Elmer Gantry for both of us.

"You don't need to think about this," he said.

"Just tell me."

"I guess it's like discovering you're on the shelf of a pawnshop, dusty and forgotten and maybe not worth very much. But Jesus comes in and tells the pawnbroker, 'I'll take her place on the shelf. Let her go outside again.'"

When I met him for a second time in his office, he handed me a quote of Dag Hammarskjöld's: "I don't know Who or What put the question, I don't know when it was put. I don't even remember answering. But at some moment, I did answer Yes." I wanted to fall to my knees, newly born, but I didn't. I walked back home to Pat's and got out the Scotch. I was feeling better in general, less out of control, even though it would be four more years before I got sober. I was not willing to give up a life of shame and failure without a fight. Still, a few weeks later, when Bill and

43

I met for our first walk, I had some progress to report: I had stopped meeting the love of my life at X-rated motels. I still met him at *motels,* but nicer ones. I had stopped seeing the man with the bleeding wife. I felt I had standards again— granted, they were very *low* standards, but still . . .

Slowly I came back to life. I'd been like one of the people Ezekiel comes upon in the valley of dry bones—people who had really given up, who were lifeless and without hope. But because of Ezekiel's presence, breath comes upon them; spirit and kindness revive them. And by the time I was well enough for Bill even to *consider* tapering off our meetings, I had weaseled my way into his heart. I drank, he led a church, and together we went walking every week all over Belvedere Island, all over the back of that great green turtle.

### Flea Market

In the dust of Marin City, a wartime settlement outside Sausalito where black shipyard workers lived during World War II, a flea market was held every weekend for years. In 1984 I was living in a mother-in-law unit on a houseboat berthed at the north end of Sausalito, on San Francisco Bay. I was almost thirty when I moved in, and I lived for the next four years in a space about ten feet square, with a sleeping loft. I had a view of the bay and of Angel Island. When it was foggy, San Francisco across the water looked like a city inside a snow globe.

I got pregnant in April, right around my thirtieth birthday, but was so loaded every night that the next morning's first urine was too diluted for a pregnancy test to prove positive. Every other day, Pammy, who still lived in Mill Valley with her husband, would come by and take a small bottle of pee to the lab that was near her home. I did not have a car. I had had a very stern conversation with myself a year before, in which I said that I had to either stop drinking or get rid of the car. This was a real no-brainer. I got around on foot, and by bus and friend.

The houseboat, on a concrete barge, barely moved even during the storms of winter. I was often sick in the mornings. On weekdays, I put coffee on, went for a run, took a shower, had coffee, maybe some speed, a thousand cigarettes, and then tried to write. On weekends, I went to the flea market.

Marin City is the ghetto in this luscious affluent county, built in a dusty bowl surrounded by low green hills on the other side of the freeway from where my houseboat was. The town is filled with families—lots of little kids and powerful mothers. There are too many drugs and guns, there is the looming and crummy government housing called the Projects, and there are six churches in a town of two thousand people who are mostly black. On the weekends, the gigantic lot where the Greyhound bus depot used to be was transformed into one of the country's biggest flea markets. Many years before, I used to sit on my mother's lap on the exact same site and watch black men drink coffee at the counter while we waited for a bus into San Francisco. Now every square foot was taken up with booths and trucks and beach umbrellas and tables and blankets and racks displaying household wares and tools and crafts and clothes, much of it stolen, most of it going for a song—hundreds of sellers, thousands of buyers, children and dogs and all of us stirring up the dust.

You could buy the most wonderful ethnic food here, food from faraway places: Asia, India, Mexico, New York City. This is where I liked to be when I was hungover or coming down off a cocaine binge, here in the dust with all these dusty people, all this liveliness and clutter and color, things for sale to cheer me up, and greasy food that would slip down my throat.

If I happened to be there between eleven and one on Sundays, I could hear gospel music coming from a church right across the street. It was called St. Andrew Presbyterian, and it looked homely and impoverished, a ramshackle building with a cross on top, sitting on a small parcel of land with a few skinny pine trees. But the music wafting out was so pretty that I would stop and listen. I knew a lot of the hymns from the times I'd gone to church with my grandparents and from the albums we'd had of spirituals. Finally, I began stopping in at St. Andrew from to time, standing in the doorway to listen to the songs. I couldn't believe how run-down it was, with terrible linoleum that was brown and overshined, and plastic stained-glass windows. But it had a choir of five black women and one rather Amish-looking white man making all that glorious noise, and a congregation of thirty people or so, radiating kindness and warmth. During the time when people hugged and greeted each other, various people would come back to where I stood to shake my hand or try to hug me; I was as frozen and stiff as Richard Nixon. After this, Scripture was read, and then the minister named James Noel who was as tall and handsome as Marvin Gaye would preach, and it would be all about social injustice—and Jesus, which would be enough to send me running back to the sanctuary of the flea market.

You'd always have to shower after you got home, you'd be so covered with dust, the soles of your shoes sticky with syrup from snow cones, or gum, or one of those small paper canoes that hot dogs are served in.

I went back to St. Andrew about once a month. No one tried to con me into sitting down or staying. I always left before the sermon. I loved singing, even about Jesus, but I just didn't want to be preached at about him. To me, Jesus made about as much sense as Scientology or dowsing. But the church smelled wonderful, like the air had nourishment in it, or like it was composed of these people's exhalations, of warmth and faith and peace. There were always children running around or being embraced, and a gorgeous stick-thin deaf black girl signing to her mother, hearing the songs and the Scripture through her mother's flashing fingers. The radical old women of the congregation were famous in these parts for having convinced the very conservative national Presbytery to donate ten thousand dollars to the Angela Davis Defense Fund during her trial up at the Civic Center. And every other week they brought huge tubs of great food for the homeless families living at the shelter near the canal to the north. I loved this. But it was the singing that pulled me in and split me wide open.

I could sing better here than I ever had before. As part of these people, even though I stayed in the doorway, I did not recognize my voice or know where it was coming from, but sometimes I felt like I could sing forever.

Eventually, a few months after I started coming, I took a seat in one of the folding chairs, off by myself. Then the singing enveloped me. It was furry and resonant, coming from everyone's very heart. There was no sense of performance or judgment, only that the music was breath and food.

Something inside me that was stiff and rotting would feel soft and tender. Somehow the singing wore down all the boundaries and distinctions that kept me so isolated. Sitting there, standing with them to sing, sometimes so shaky and sick that I felt like I might tip over, I felt bigger than myself, like I was being taken care of, tricked into coming back to life. But I had to leave before the sermon.

That April of 1984, in the midst of this experience, Pammy took a fourth urine sample to the lab, and it finally came back positive. I had published three books by then, but none of them had sold particularly well, and I did not have the money or wherewithal to have a baby. The father was someone I had just met, who was married, and no one I wanted a real life or baby with. So Pammy one evening took me in for the abortion, and I was sadder than I'd been since my father died, and when she brought me home that night, I went upstairs to my loft with a pint of Bushmills and some of the codeine a nurse had given me for pain. I drank until nearly dawn.

Then the next night I did it again, and the next night, although by then the pills were gone.

I didn't go to the flea market the week of my abortion. I stayed home, and smoked dope and got drunk, and tried to write a little, and went for slow walks along the salt marsh with Pammy. On the seventh night, though, very drunk and just about to take a sleeping pill, I discovered that I was bleeding heavily. It did not stop over the next hour. I was going through a pad every fifteen minutes, and I thought I should call a doctor or Pammy, but I was so disgusted that I had gotten so drunk one week after an abortion that I just couldn't wake someone up and ask for help. I kept on changing Kotex, and I got very sober very quickly. Several hours later, the blood stopped flowing, and I got in bed, shaky and sad and too wild to have another drink or take a sleeping pill. I had a cigarette and turned off the light. After a while, as I lay there, I became aware of someone with me, hunkered down in the corner, and I just assumed it was my father, whose presence I had felt over the years when I was frightened and alone. The feeling was so strong that I actually turned on the light for a moment to make sure no one was there—of course, there wasn't. But after a while, in the dark again, I knew beyond any doubt that it was Jesus. I felt him as surely as I feel my dog lying nearby as I write this.

And I was appalled. I thought about my life and my brilliant hilarious progressive friends, I thought about what everyone would think of me if I became a Christian, and it seemed an utterly impossible thing that simply could not be allowed to happen. I turned to the wall and said out loud, "I would rather die."

I felt him just sitting there on his haunches in the corner of my sleeping loft, watching me with patience and love, and I squinched my eyes shut, but that didn't help because that's not what I was seeing him with.

Finally I fell asleep, and in the morning, he was gone.

This experience spooked me badly, but I thought it was just an apparition, born of fear and self-loathing and booze and loss of blood. But then everywhere I went, I had the feeling that a little cat was following me, wanting me to reach down and pick it up, wanting me to open the door and let it in. But I knew what would happen: you let a cat in one time, give it a little milk, and then it stays forever. So I tried to keep one step ahead of it, slamming my houseboat door when I entered or left.

And one week later, when I went back to church, I was so hungover that I couldn't stand up for the songs, and this time I stayed for the sermon, which I just thought was so ridiculous, like someone trying to convince me of the existence of extraterrestrials, but the last song was so deep and raw and pure that I could not escape. It was as if the people were singing in between the notes, weeping and joyful at the same time, and I felt like their voices or *something* was rocking me in its bosom, holding me like a scared kid, and I opened up to that feeling—and it washed over me.

I began to cry and left before the benediction, and I raced home and felt the little cat running along at my heels, and I walked down the dock past dozens of potted flowers, under a sky as blue as one of God's own dreams, and I opened the door to my houseboat, and I stood there a minute, and then I hung my head and said, "Fuck it: I quit." I took a long deep breath and said out loud, "All right. You can come in."

So this was my beautiful moment of conversion.

*And here in dust and dirt, O here,*
*The lilies of his love appear.*

I started to find these lines of George Herbert's everywhere I turned—in Simone Weil, Malcolm Muggeridge,
books of English poetry. Meanwhile, I trooped back and
forth through the dust and grime of the flea market every
Sunday morning till eleven, when I crossed the street from
the market to the church.

I was sitting through the sermon now every week and
finding that I could not only bear the Jesus talk but was
interested, searching for clues. I was more and more comfortable with the radical message of peace and equality,
with the God in whom Dr. King believed. I had no big theological thoughts but had discovered that if I said, Hello?,
to God, I could *feel* God say, Hello, back. It was like being
in a relationship with Casper. Sometimes I wadded up a
Kleenex and held it tightly in one fist so that it felt like I was
walking hand and hand with him.

Finally, one morning in July of 1986, I woke up so sick
and in such despair for the umpteenth day in a row that I
knew that I was either going to die or have to quit drinking.
I poured a bottle of pinot noir down the sink, and dumped
a Nike box full of assorted pills off the side of my houseboat, and entered into recovery with fear and trembling. I
was not sure that I could or even wanted to go one day
without drinking or pills or cocaine. But it turned out that
I could and that a whole lot of people were going to help
me, with kind eyes and hot cups of bad coffee.

If I were to give a slide show of the next ten years, it
would begin on the day I was baptized, one year after I got

sober. I called Reverend Noel at eight that morning and told him that I really didn't think I was ready because I wasn't good enough yet. Also, I was insane. My heart was good, but my insides had gone bad. And he said, "You're putting the cart before the horse. So—honey? Come on *down*." My family and all my closest friends came to church that day to watch as James dipped his hand into the font, bathed my forehead with cool water, and spoke the words of Langston Hughes:

> *Gather out of star-dust*
> *Earth-dust,*
> *Cloud-dust,*
> *Storm-dust,*
> *And splinters of hail,*
> *One handful of dream-dust*
> *Not for sale.*

In the next slide, two years later, I'm pregnant by a man I was dating, who really didn't want to be a father at the time. I was still poor, but friends and the people at my church convinced me that if I decided to have a child, we would be provided for every step of the way. Pammy really wanted the kid. She had been both trying to conceive and waiting to adopt for years. She said, "Let me put it this way, Annie. We're going to have this baby."

In the next slide, in August of 1989, my son is born. I named him Sam. He had huge eyes and his father's straight hair. Three months later he was baptized at St. Andrew.

Then, six months later, there would be a slide of me

nursing Sam, holding the phone to my ear with a look of shock on my face, because Pammy had just been diagnosed with metastatic breast cancer. She had a lumpectomy and then aggressive chemotherapy. All that platinum hair fell out, and she took to wearing beautiful scarves and soft cotton caps. I would show you a slide of her dancing in a ballet group for breast cancer survivors. I would show you a slide of her wading in the creek at Samuel P. Taylor Park, her jeans rolled up and Sam, on her shoulders, holding on to the ends of her scarf like reins. There was joy and there were many setbacks, and she played it way down: two days after she'd finally begun to complain mildly about a cough that wouldn't go away, a doctor aspirated a *liter* of fluid from her lungs. More chemo, and the hair that had grown back fell out again. "Come shave it all off for me," she asked over the phone. "As it is, it looks like hair I found in the trash can and tried to glue back on." I gently brushed almost all of it off. She loved visits with Sam, grieved that she wouldn't get to watch him grow older. The cancer went into remission. A few months later, a slide would show her in a soft pink cotton cap with a look of supreme joy on her face, because her adoption lawyer had finally called and asked if she and her husband wanted to adopt. They did. They were given a baby girl named Rebecca, my darling goddaughter.

But the cancer came back. Not long before she died, my favorite slide would show her lying on a chaise in her lush and overgrown garden, beaming. Out of a storage room that we used for changing Rebecca, we had just fashioned a guest room for her sister, who was coming in from Italy to take care of her. She'd been up and around all morning, trying out the guest bed here and then there, putting it near the window, wanting the sun to fall on her sister just so. We found a place for all the extra junk, and a little rug for the floor, a tiny chest of drawers, and pictures for the wall. So then she went outside to rest, dressed, happy, looking once more like a citizen of the world. It was sunny and blue, a perfect day, and she had the radiance of someone who has been upright and really moving for one last time, so happy and light that even without hair, wearing a scarf, she seemed like a blonde again.

She was thirty-seven when she died. We scattered her ashes one sunny day from a boat out near the Farallon Islands—white-gold sunlight, mild breezes, baskets and bags of roses.

Then there would be some fabulous slides of Rebecca growing up. In many of these photos, she is dressed in bright saris and veils, as she and her dad go to India quite a lot to visit an ashram there. She has long brown hair, like a filly.

Meanwhile, Sam grew tall and thin and sweet, with huge brown eyes.

Then there would be thousands of slides of Sam and me at St. Andrew. I think we have missed church ten times in twelve years. Sam would be snuggled in people's arms in the earlier shots, shyly trying to wriggle free of hugs in the later ones. There would be different pastors along the way, none of them exactly right for us until a few years ago when a tall African-American woman named Veronica came to lead us. She has huge gentle doctor hands, with dimples where the knuckles should be, like a baby's fists. She stepped into us, the wonderful old worn pair of pants that is St. Andrew, and they fit. She sings to us sometimes from the pulpit and tells us stories of when she was a child. She told us this story just the other day: When she was about seven, her best friend got lost one day. The little girl ran up and down the streets of the big town where they lived, but she couldn't find a single landmark. She was very frightened. Finally a policeman stopped to help her. He put her in the passenger seat of his car, and they drove around until she finally saw her church. She pointed it out to the policeman, and then she told him firmly, "You could let me out now. This is my church, and I can always find my way home from here."

And that is why I have stayed so close to mine—because no matter how bad I am feeling, how lost or lonely or frightened, when I see the faces of the people at my church, and hear their tawny voices, I can always find my way home.

# Part One

# MOUNTAIN, VALLEY, SKY

Except for the point, the still point,
There would be no dance,
and there is only the dance.

T. S. ELIOT

# KNOCKING ON HEAVEN'S DOOR

So there I was on a plane returning home from St. Louis. Or rather, there I was in a plane on the runway at the airport in St. Louis with, I think, the not unreasonable expectation that we would be in the air soon, as our flight had already been delayed two hours. I was anxious to get home, as I had not seen Sam in several days, but all things considered, I thought I was coping quite well, especially because I am a skeptical and terrified flier. In between devouring Hershey's chocolate and thirteen dollars' worth of trashy magazines, I had spent the two hours of the delay trying to be helpful to the other stranded passengers: I distributed all my magazines and most of my chocolates; I got an old man some water; I flirted with the babies; I mingled, I schmoozed. I had recently seen what may have been a miracle at my church and had been feeling ever since that I was supposed to walk through life with a deeper faith, a deeper assurance that if I took care of God's children for God, he or she would take care of me. So I took care of people, and hoped that once we were on board, everything would go smoothly.

My idea of everything going smoothly on an airplane is (a) that I not die in a slow-motion fiery crash or get stabbed to death by terrorists and (b) that none of the other passengers try to talk to me. All conversation should end at the moment the wheels leave the ground.

Finally we were allowed to board. I was in row thirty-eight, between a woman slightly older than I, with limited language skills, and a man my own age who was reading a book by a famous right-wing Christian novelist about the Apocalypse. A newspaper had asked me to review this book when it first came out, because its author and I are both Christians—although as I pointed out in my review, he's one of those right-wing Christians who thinks that Jesus is coming back next Tuesday right after lunch, and I am one of those left-wing Christians who thinks that perhaps this author is just spiritualizing his own hysteria.

"How is it?" I asked, pointing jovially to the man's book, partly to be friendly, partly to gauge where he stood politically.

"This is one of the best books I've ever read," he replied. "You should read it." I nodded. I remembered saying in the review that the book was hard-core right-wing paranoid anti-Semitic homophobic misogynistic propaganda—not to put too fine a point on it. The man smiled and went back to reading.

I couldn't begin to guess what country the woman was from, although I think it's possible that she had one Latvian parent and one Korean. She sounded a little like Latka Gravas, the Andy Kaufman character on *Taxi*, except after things began to fall apart, when she sounded just like the martians in *Mars Attacks:* "Ack ack ack!" she'd cry. But I'm getting ahead of myself.

As we sat there on the runway, the man with the book about the Apocalypse commented on the small gold cross I wear.

"Are you born again?" he asked, as we taxied down the runway. He was rather prim and tense, maybe a little like David Eisenhower with a spastic colon. I did not know how to answer for a moment.

"Yes," I said. "I am."

My friends like to tell each other that I am not really a born-again Christian. They think of me more along the lines of that old Jonathan Miller routine, where he said, "I'm not really a Jew—I'm Jew-ish." They think I am Christian-ish. But I'm not. I'm just a bad Christian. A bad born-again Christian. And certainly, like the apostle Peter, I am capable of denying it, of presenting myself as a sort of leftist liberation-theology enthusiast and maybe sort of a vaguely Jesusy bon vivant. But it's not true. And I believe that when you get on a plane, if you start lying you are totally doomed.

So I told the truth: that I am a believer, a convert. I'm probably about three months away from slapping an aluminum Jesus-fish on the back of my car, although I first want to see if the application or stickum in any way interferes with my lease agreement. And believe me, all this boggles even *my* mind. But it's true. I could go to a gathering of foot-wash Baptists and, except for my dreadlocks, fit right in. I would wash their feet; I would let them wash mine.

But as the plane taxied out to the runway, the man on

my right began telling me how he and his wife were home-schooling their children, and he described with enormous acrimony the radical, free-for-all, feminist, touchy-feely philosophy of his county's school system, and I knew instantly that this description was an act of aggression against me—that he was telepathically on to me, could see that I was the enemy, that I will be on the same curling team in heaven as Tom Hayden and Vanessa Redgrave. And then suddenly the plane braked to a stop.

We all looked around for a moment, before the captain came on the P. A. system and announced calmly that two passengers wanted to get off the plane, right then and there. We were headed back to the gate. "What?" we all cried. The good news was that this was only going to take a minute or so, since in the past two hours we had only traveled about five hundred feet. The bad news was that FAA regulations required that security go over all of the stowed luggage to make sure these two people had not accidentally left behind their pipe bombs.

The Latvian woman stared at me quizzically. I explained very slowly and very loudly what was going on. She gaped at me for a long moment. "Ack," she whispered.

Eventually the three of us in row thirty-eight began to read. The other two seemed resigned, but I felt frantic, like I might develop a blinky facial tic at any moment. Time passed underwater.

An hour later the plane finally took off.

We, the citizens of row thirty-eight, all ordered sodas. The Latvian woman put on a Walkman and began to listen with her eyes closed; the Christian man read his book about the Apocalypse; I read *The New Yorker*. Then the seat-belt sign came on, and the pilot's voice came back over the P. A. system. "I'm afraid we are about to hit some heavy turbulence," he said. "Please return to your seats."

The next minute the plane was bouncing around so hard that we had to hold on to our drinks. "Ack ack ack!" said the Latvian, grabbing for her Sprite.

"Everyone take your seat," the pilot barked over the P. A. system. "We are in for some rough going." My heart thumped around my chest like a tennis shoe in the dryer.

The plane rose and fell and shook, and the pilot came back on and said sternly, like an angry dad, "Flight attendants, sit down *now*!" And the plane hit huge waves and currents on the choppy sea of sky, and we bounced and moaned and gasped. "Whhhoooooaaaa!" we said as one, as though we were on a roller-coaster ride. We're going down, I thought. I know that a basic tenet of the Christian faith is that death is really just a major change of address, but I had to close my eyes to squinch back tears of terror and loss. Oh, my God, I thought, oh, my God: I'll never see Sam again. This will kill me a second time. The plane bucked and shook without stopping and the Christian man read calmly, stoically, rather pleased with his composure, it seemed to my tiny, hysterical self. The Latvian closed her eyes and turned up her Walkman. I could hear it softly. And I, praying for a miracle, thought about the miracle I had seen in church.

One of our newer members, a man named Ken Nelson, is dying of AIDS, disintegrating before our very eyes. He came in a year ago with a Jewish woman who comes every week to be with us, although she does not believe in Jesus. Shortly after the man with AIDS started coming, his partner died of the disease. A few weeks later Ken told us that right after Brandon died, Jesus had slid into the hole in his heart that Brandon's loss left, and had been there ever since. Ken has a totally lopsided face, ravaged and emaciated, but when he smiles, he is radiant. He looks like God's crazy nephew Phil. He says that he would gladly pay any price for what he has now, which is Jesus, and us.

There's a woman in the choir named Ranola who is large and beautiful and jovial and black and as devout as can be, who has been a little standoffish toward Ken. She has always looked at him with confusion, when she looks at him at all. Or she looks at him sideways, as if she wouldn't have to quite see him if she didn't look at him head on. She was raised in the South by Baptists who taught her that his way of life—that he—was an abomination. It is hard for her to break through this. I think she and a few other women at church are, on the most visceral level, a little afraid of catching the disease. But Kenny has come to church almost every week for the last year and won almost everyone over. He finally missed a couple of Sundays when he got too weak, and then a month ago he was back, weighing almost no pounds, his face even more lopsided, as if he'd had a stroke. Still, during the prayers of the people, he talked joyously of his life and his decline, of grace and redemption, of how safe and happy he feels these days.

So on this one particular Sunday, for the first hymn, the so-called Morning Hymn, we sang "Jacob's Ladder," which goes, "Every rung goes higher, higher," while ironically

Kenny couldn't even stand up. But he sang away sitting down, with the hymnal in his lap. And then when it came time for the second hymn, the Fellowship Hymn, we were to sing "His Eye Is on the Sparrow." The pianist was playing and the whole congregation had risen—only Ken remained seated, holding the hymnal in his lap—and we began to sing, "Why should I feel discouraged? Why do the shadows fall?" And Ranola watched Ken rather skeptically for a moment, and then her face began to melt and contort like his, and she went to his side and bent down to lift him up—lifted up this white rag doll, this scarecrow. She held him next to her, draped over and against her like a child while they sang. And it pierced me.

I can't imagine anything but music that could have brought about this alchemy. Maybe it's because music is about as physical as it gets: your essential rhythm is your heartbeat; your essential sound, the breath. We're walking temples of noise, and when you add tender hearts to this mix, it somehow lets us meet in places we couldn't get to any other way.

Meanwhile, little by little, the plane grew steadier, and the pilot announced that everything was OK. I was so excited that we were not going to crash and that I might actually get to see Sam again that I started feeling mingly, suddenly wanted the Christian man to be my new best friend. But just as I opened my mouth, the pilot came back once more to ask if there was a doctor on board.

The woman behind us, who turned out to be a nurse, got up and went back to investigate. The Christian man prayed; I tried to rubberneck, but I couldn't see a thing. I went back to thinking about Ken and my church and how on that Sunday, Ranola and Ken, of whom she was so afraid, were trying to sing. He looked like a child who was singing simply because small children sing all the time—they haven't made the separation between speech and music. Then both Ken and Ranola began to cry. Tears were pouring down their faces, and their noses were running like rivers, but as she held him up, she suddenly lay her black weeping face against his feverish white one, put her face right up against his and let all those spooky fluids mingle with hers.

When the nurse sitting behind us returned, she offered the news that a woman in the back was having a heart attack. A heart attack! But there were doctors on hand, and the nurse thought the woman was going to be OK.

"Good Lord," said the Christian man. We looked at each other and sighed, and shook our heads, and continued to look at each other.

"God," I said. "I just hope the snakes don't get out of the cargo hold next." The prim apocalyptic man smiled. Then he laughed out loud. The Latvian woman started laughing, although she still had her Walkman on, and while I hate to look like I'm enjoying my own jokes too much, I started laughing too. The three of us sat there in hysterics, and when we were done, the man reached over and patted the back of my hand, smiling gently. The Latvian woman leaned in close to me, into my Soviet air space, and beamed. I leaned forward so that our foreheads touched for just a second. I thought, I do not know if what happened at church was an honest-to-God little miracle, and I don't know if there has been another one here, the smallest possible sort, the size of a tiny bird, but I feel like I am sitting with my cousins on a plane eight miles up, a plane that is going to make it home—and this made me so happy that I suddenly thought, This is plenty of miracle for me to rest in now.

# LADDERS

In May of 1992 I went to Ixtapa with Sam, who was then two and a half. At the time, Pammy had been battling breast cancer for two years. I also had a boyfriend with whom I spoke two or three times a day, whom I loved and who loved me. Then in early November of that year, the big eraser came down and got Pammy, and it also got the boyfriend, from whom I parted by mutual agreement. The grief was huge, monolithic.

All those years I fell for the great palace lie that grief should be gotten over as quickly as possible and as privately. But what I've discovered since is that the lifelong fear of grief keeps us in a barren, isolated place and that only grieving can heal grief; the passage of time will lessen the acuteness, but time alone, without the direct experience of grief, will not heal it. San Francisco is a city in grief, we are a world in grief, and it is at once intolerable and a great opportunity. I'm pretty sure that it is only by experiencing that ocean of sadness in a naked and immediate way that we come to be healed—which is to say, that we come to experience life with a real sense of presence and spaciousness and peace. I began to learn this when Sam and I went back to the same resort three months after Pammy's death.

I took him back partly for reasons of punctuation. He was different this time, though. We both were. I had discovered that I could just barely live without Pammy. Every time I went back to her house to visit her daughter, Rebecca, I heard Pammy's flute, remembered exactly the yellow of her hair, felt stalked by her absence, noted by it. It was like the hot yellow day that Faulkner describes in *Light in August* as "a prone and somnolent yellow cat," contemplating the narrator. At any moment, the cat might suddenly spring.

Also, I was a little angry with men at the time, and scared; in the aftermath of the romantic loss, my heart felt like it had a fence surrounding it. Now Sam seemed to be standing with me behind this fence; he seemed to feel safe only around me. He was sweet and friendly but shyer, no longer the social butterfly he had been the year before when Pammy had still been alive. Back then I could leave him all day in the resort's child-care program. This time he was clingy and heavily Oedipal. I began to call myself Jocasta; he began to call me darling.

The first year, I'd come here alone with Sam. I swam and ate by myself most of the time, walking into the dining area three times a day feeling shy and odd, cringing, with my arms stiffly at my side like Pee-Wee Herman. But this year I was with my friend Tom, an extremely funny Jesuit and sober alcoholic, who drank like a rat for years and smoked a little non-habit-forming marijuana on a daily basis. He also did amyl nitrate, although he adds that this was just to get to know people.

His best friend Pat was along, too. I found that I could hardly stand for people to have best friends who were still alive. But when Sam and I had breakfast with both of them at the airport the morning we left, they made me laugh and forget myself.

Pat is a very pretty woman in her late forties who is about a hundred pounds overweight, and sober seven years.

"Pat has a *lot* of problems," Tom told us over breakfast.

"This is true," said Pat.

"She was sober for four years," he continued, "until her husband got brain cancer. Then for a few years she had a little social Tylenol with codeine every day, with the merest slug of Nyquil every night for a cold that just wouldn't go away."

"I was a little depressed," she said.

After breakfast, we flew to Ixtapa. Adobe haciendas, cobblestone paths, a long white beach, palm trees, bougainvillea, warm ocean water—and no one back home desperately hoping I'd call.

Grief, as I read somewhere once, is a lazy Susan. One day it is heavy and underwater, and the next day it spins and stops at loud and rageful, and the next day at wounded keening, and the next day numbness, silence. I was hoarse for the first six weeks after Pammy died and my romance ended, from shouting in the car and crying, and I had blisters on the palm of one hand from hitting the bed with my tennis racket, bellowing in pain and anger. But on the first morning in Mexico, the lazy Susan stopped at feelings of homesickness, like when my parents sold the house where I grew up.

I woke before Sam and lay in my bed in the cool, white adobe room, filled with memories of my first day here the year before. I remembered calling Pammy and my lover that first morning, how they gasped with pleasure to hear my voice. I lay there thinking this time that I had made a dreadful mistake to return, that I was not ready to laugh or play or even relax, and I wondered whether or not God had yet another rabbit he or she could pull out of the hat. Then my Oedipal little son woke up and hopped over to my bed. He patted my face for a while and said tenderly, "You're a beautiful girl."

The year before, when I dropped him off at the thatched child-care unit, we'd walk holding hands, and on the way he'd cry out joyfully, "Hi, Sky, my name is Sam. I yike you," because he couldn't say his *l*'s. "Hi, Yeaf," he'd say happily to the leaves, "my name is Sam. I yike you." It seemed very long ago. This year he looked at me all the time like a mournful finacé and said, "I want to kiss you on the yips."

On the third day in Mexico Tom told me that Jung, some time after his beloved wife died, said, "It cost me a great deal to regain my footing. Now I am free to become who I truly am." And this is God's own truth: the more often I cried in my room in Ixtapa and felt just generally wretched, the more often I started to have occasional moments of utter joy, of feeling aware of each moment shining for its own momentous sake. I am no longer convinced that you're *supposed* to get over the death of certain people, but little by little, pale and swollen around the eyes, I began to feel a sense of reception, that I was beginning to receive the fact of Pammy's death, the finality. I let it enter me.

I was terribly erratic: feeling so holy and serene some moments that I was sure I was going to end up dating the Dalai Lama. Then the grief and craziness would hit again, and I would be in Broken Mind, back in the howl.

The depth of the feeling continued to surprise and threaten me, but each time it hit again and I bore it, like a nicotine craving, I would discover that it hadn't washed me away. After a while it was like an inside shower, washing off some of the rust and calcification in my pipes. It was like giving a dry garden a good watering. Don't get me wrong: grief sucks; it really does. Unfortunately, though, avoiding it robs us of life, of the now, of a sense of living spirit. Mostly I have tried to avoid it by staying very busy, working too hard, trying to achieve as much as possible. You can often avoid the pain by trying to fix other people; shopping helps in a pinch, as does romantic obsession. Martyrdom can't be beat. While too much exercise works for many people, it doesn't for me, but I have found that a stack of magazines can be numbing and even mood altering. But the bad news is that whatever you use to keep the pain at bay robs you of the flecks and nuggets of gold that feeling grief will give you. A fixation can keep you nicely defined and give you the illusion that your life has not fallen apart. But since your life may indeed have fallen apart, the illusion won't hold up forever, and if you are lucky and brave, you will be willing to bear disillusion. You begin to cry and writhe and yell and then to keep on crying; and then, finally, grief ends up giving you the two best things: softness and illumination.

Every afternoon when I'd pick Sam up at the kids' club, it was as if he'd spent the day in a workshop on Surviving the Loss of Your Mother. When I'd appear Lazarus-like to take him back to our room, his joy was huge. We always stopped to watch the iguanas who gathered on the grass near the lagoon, the giant adults like something out of *Jurassic Park,* the babies from Dr. Seuss. They were so wonderfully absurd and antediluvian that it was like communion between you and them and something ancient.

We spent a lot of time in our room, too. It was air-conditioned. Sam, so solemn and watchful, frequently brought up the last time he had seen Pammy, on Halloween, three days before she died. He was dressed up as a sea monster, and he sat on her bed and they sang "Frère Jacques" together. He went over and over the facts of the evening: "She was in her jammies?" "Yes." "I was in my sea monster costume?" "That's right." I thought a lot about the effect of Pammy's death on Sam, my own stunned attempts to deal with that, the worry that he voiced every few days that if *Rebecca*'s mother could die, then wasn't it possible that his could too? I somehow felt that all I had to offer was my own willingness to feel bad. I figured that eventually the plates of the earth would shift inside me, and I would feel a lessening of the pain. Trying to fix him, or distract him, or jolly him out of his depression would actually be a disservice. I prayed for the willingness to let him feel sad and displaced until he was able to stop slogging through the confusion and step back into the river of ordinariness. The sun beat down, the hours passed slowly to the drone of the air conditioner. I kept starting to cry and then falling asleep. Sometimes grief looks like narcolepsy.

One afternoon in our room I had been crying a little while Sam dozed in his own bed. Then I fell deeply asleep. I woke much later to find Sam standing by my bed, tugging at my sleeve, looking at me earnestly with his huge googily extraterrestrial eyes. He cleared his throat and then said something I guess he must have heard on TV. He said, "Excuse me, mister."

It made my heart hurt. I thought I was going to die. In "Song of Myself," Whitman wrote, "Sometimes touching another person is more than I can bear."

There was a man here this time with just one leg. I'd seen his prosthetic leg lying around by the pool a few times before I actually saw him, and when I did, he was climbing up a trapeze ladder in the circus grounds. Circus school was held every afternoon at three on the lawn between the haciendas and the beach, using an elaborate rig of ropes and swings and netting. The man was wearing shorts, and his stump was visible an inch or two below the hemline—and I've got to say that this kicked the shit out of my feeling self-conscious in shorts because of my cellulite and stretch marks.

He climbed the ladder with disjointed grace, asymmetrical but not clumsy, rung by rung, focused and steady and slow. Then he reached the platform, put on his safety harness, and swung out over the safety net, his one leg hooked over the bar of the trapeze, swinging back and forth, and finally letting go. A teacher on the other trapeze swung toward him, and they caught each other's hands and held on, and they swung back and forth for a while. Then he dropped on his back to the safety net and raised his fist in victory. "Yes," he said, and lay there on the net for a long time, looking at the sky with a secret smile.

I approached him shyly at lunch the next day and said, "You were great on the trapeze. Are you going to do it again?" And I had this idea that he might so that I could do some serious writing about spirit and guts and triumph. But all he said was "Honey? I got much bigger mountains to climb."

Life does not seem to present itself to me for my convenience, to box itself up nicely so I can write about it with wisdom and a point to make before putting it on a shelf somewhere. Now, in my early forties, I understand just enough about life to understand that I do not understand much of anything. You show me a man with one leg climbing up a trapeze ladder, and the best I can do is to tell you that when I saw him, he was *very* focused and in a good mood.

The next day I saw his plastic leg lying on a beach towel at the far end of the beach, where the wind-surfing lessons take place. Oh, dear, I thought. The shoelace of the expensive sneaker on the foot of the plastic leg was untied. I went and tied it, and then sat down in the sand. I really wanted to ask how he lost his leg and how he got back on his feet, when one was now made of plastic. I remembered how, a few months before Pammy died, we read a line by the great

Persian mystical poet Rumi: "Where there is ruin, there is hope for a treasure." Pammy and I talked at the time of a sunken ship on the bottom of the ocean, full of jewels and gold; it was there in the heightened sense of existence and of the sacred that we felt in the midst of the devastation of her illness. It was there in the incredible sense of immediacy and joy we had felt some days toward the end, cruising malls and parks, Pammy in her wheelchair, wearing a wig, lashing me with a blue silken scarf to go faster. I sat on the beach hoping to see the man again, thinking of how much we lose yet how much remains, but it was getting late and I needed to go pick up Sam, and I left before the man with one leg returned.

My new friend Pat had gone snorkeling almost every afternoon and loved it more than any other activity, although because of her weight it was impossible for her to climb back into the boat unaided. On the day before we left Mexico, I decided to give it a try. The snorkel boat left at three every day and took a group of people across the bay to a cove twenty minutes away. Over lunch, though, I started to chicken out, until Pat said I had to go, that we couldn't be friends if I didn't. "Then tell me what you love most about it, "I said. She thought for a while, and then a faraway, almost sensuous look came over her face. "I like picking out the guys who are going to help push my big, wet, slippery body back up the ladder onto the boat," she said slowly.

Tom and I ended up going together. The little cove was near a beach with grass huts and umbrellas on the white sands; cactuses on ancient neighboring hills framed it all.

We donned our gear and jumped in. The water is not crystal clear, and there are not a million brilliantly colored fish to watch, but if there is a heaven—and I think there really may be one—it may be similar to snorkeling: dreamy, soft, bright, quiet.

At first my breath underwater sounded labored and congested, like the Keir Dullea character's in *2001* when he's in the pod outside the mother ship. I floated off by myself. Then in the silence I felt for a while as if I were breathing along with everything in the world. It is such a nice break from real life not to have to weigh anything. Beautiful green plants swayed in the current, funny little fish floated past.

I daydreamed about Pammy. Near the end, she said of her young daughter, "All I have to do to get really depressed is to think about Rebecca, and all I have to do to get really joyful is to think about Rebecca." I floated around slowly, crying; the mask filled up with tears—I could have used a windshield wiper. I felt very lonely. I thought maybe I wouldn't feel so bad if I didn't have such big pieces of Pammy still inside me, but then I thought, I want those pieces in me for the rest of my life, whatever it costs me. So I floated along, still feeling lonely but now not quite so adrift because I starting thinking of Pat, big and fat and brave enough to wear a swimsuit in front of us. I laughed, remembering what she'd said about the ladder, and I accidentally swallowed water. I watched the small fish swim in and out of the feathery sea plants, and I thought of beautiful wild happy Rebecca. This made my heart hurt too, yet I began to feel a little lighter inside. And just then Tom came paddling over, and I became aware of his presence beside me although I couldn't actually see his face, and for the longest time we lay there bobbing on the water's surface, face down, lost in our own worlds, barely moving our fins, side by side.

# MOUNTAIN BIRTHDAY

T wo days before his seventh birthday, Sam and I were in a town in Idaho, several thousand feet above sea level, where I was teaching at a writing conference. We were taking an early morning walk in a valley that was so majestic it made you feel patriotic, when Sam noticed half a dozen paragliders floating down off the jagged high mountain above us. His eyes radiated excitement, because a friend of ours routinely paraglides off the cliffs near Santa Cruz and had been promising him for a while now that he could go paragliding in a tandem harness when he was just a bit bigger—and here he was about to turn *seven*. So we stopped and looked skyward, in postures of reverence and awe. Partly we were blown away by the beauty of the mountain and the sky. And partly our mouths were hanging open because these fabulous silk-winged creatures— wings of aqua, lavender, rose, apricot, red—were hanging in the sky above us, like a little sky gang led by Icarus himself.

After a minute, when it became clear that they were going to land a few hundred feet away, Sam begged me to run with him to their landing spot. "Please, please," he called over his shoulder as he ran toward them, "help me this *one* time. I've got to talk to them." So I followed along behind him.

This is what happened: a man landed at our feet a moment later. Sam stared up into his face like Jesus or Jim Carrey had just appeared, and the pilot smiled at him and shook his hand. "My birthday is in two days," said Sam, as the man gathered up the purple silk wing.

"Really!" said the pilot. "Well, what if I took you up in a harness with me, to celebrate? I've been taking my boy out since he was five. How about it, Mom?"

Now, first of all I hate being called "Mom" by grown men. Second, I am not the bravest mother on earth, and I was immediately torn about what to do. The man gave me his business card. He was the owner of a local paragliding outfit, as well as an instructor and, according to the card, a tandem specialist. He said he would love to take *both* of us on complimentary tandem paragliding rides two mornings later.

"Whoa, whoa, great," Sam said. "Whoa! Great!" But I told the instructor that we'd think about it, that he could tentatively save the early morning spot on August 29 for Sam, and we would get back to him. But I already knew that I didn't want to go. I do not have any illusions that I would make a good paraglider. What confused me, however, was how much freedom I was supposed to give Sam. I'm unclear about the fine line between good parenting and being overly protective. I get stumped by the easy test questions—like whether I should let Sam ride his two-wheeler for several blocks without me when I secretly want to run alongside him like a golden retriever. He wants to walk to a friend's house; I want him to stay inside and draw while I sit on the front porch with a shotgun across my lap like Granny Clampett.

Unfortunately, we have no front porch.

So what I needed to know up there in that beautiful valley was would a normal person—if there is such a thing as a normal person—feel that it was a good idea for a seven-year-old to paraglide in a harness with a tandem expert off a mountain fifteen hundred feet up.

Needless to say, there was no one around remotely fitting the description of a normal person: I was at a *writing* conference. Sam desperately wanted to go. He begged me to let him keep the appointment, to let him go up to that mountain, step off into thin air, and wait for the moment when the air underneath fills the wings of the paraglider and allows one to soar. And I kept thinking that maybe it was meant to be: the paraglide pilot had, after all, landed virtually—and successfully—at our feet and had offered Sam a spectacular present that would more than make up for the fact that Sam was a thousand miles away from home and all his friends on his birthday.

Later that afternoon, Sam looked up at me beseechingly and said, "It has always been a dream of mine to fly." I stared at him and thought, Oh, dear, he has begun channeling John Kennedy. Then I tried to figure out what to do. I would decide one thing—to let him fly, to give him his freedom, his wings. I'd remind myself that I usually feel deeply and philosophically that Sam is not mine, or at any rate, that he is not my chattel—that he is on loan, he belongs to God, but for whatever reason, he has been entrusted to my care—entrusted, rather, to my clutches. Then I would decide that I was crazy, that the world is aquiver with menace as it is, and one does not need to exacerbate this state of affairs by flinging one's own child off a mountain.

Later that afternoon I went to sit alone by the river. Cottonwood fluffs flocked upward through the sunbeams as if hearing a call, and children ran along the edge of the river like little bankers, gathering stones and pebbles, grasses and twigs. I prayed to know what to do, and I kept thinking I was hearing an answer, but it was like a one-woman Ping-Pong game: I decided he could go, I decided he couldn't, I decided he could. I realized that I was getting crazier with every passing moment, and that since you can't heal your own sick mind *with* your own sick mind, I needed to consult somebody else's sick mind. So I called all of my smartest friends.

Half said I should let Sam go, half acted as if I were considering buying Sam a chain saw for his birthday. But all the ones who believe in God told me to pray, so I did. Here are the two best prayers I know: "Help me, help me, help me," and "Thank you, thank you, thank you." A woman I know says, for her morning prayer, "Whatever," and then for the evening, "Oh, well," but has conceded that these prayers are more palatable for people without children.

Needless to say, I still didn't know what to do.

The next morning, the day before Sam's birthday, I was still lying in bed when I remembered an anonymous poem I've seen several times over the years. It says that after we jump into the darkness of the unknown, faith lets us believe that we will either land on solid ground, or we will be taught how to fly—and I spent some time trying to figure out whether this meant Sam would land safely or that after he crashed, his spirit would rise up out of the pile of mush he had become and fly off to be with Jesus and Pammy in heaven. Maybe it's not really all that big a deal to him, I thought wishfully, but moments later Sam got out of his bed, came over to mine, and got down on his knees. He bowed down before me. "Pleeeeeeeassssse," he moaned, "pleeeeeeeeaaassssse."

I told him I hadn't made a decision. He sighed. "It's not such a very big mountain," he implored. Then he tried sweet talk. I became "wonderful perfect thin mother," as in "Let me get you some water, wonderful perfect thin mother." Next he tried guilt mongering: when I snapped at him to stop pestering me about it, he managed to look exactly like Stan Laurel for a moment and then said, "I wish I'd been given a mother who *liked* children." After breakfast, he went off to swim with a friend, and I went outside to look at the mountain peak in daylight. Maybe Sam was right, I thought, it wasn't such a very big mountain. But it was. I saw something very imposing, masculine, American—a craggy snow-covered peak. Hillsides swelled beneath it like well-defined muscles.

I remembered the old line that if you want to make God laugh, tell her your plans. But I also heard these words in my head: seek wise counsel.

So at dinner that night, on an expanse of lawn beneath the mountain, I sat down between two older people, a brilliant Zen adventure writer and his marvelous wife. I told them about the pilot's offer and how we had tentatively accepted. Even before I'd filled in all the details, the wife was shaking her head. She said, "This is a very bad idea. You must not do it. He is too small. He has a lifetime of adventures ahead of him." The husband listened to her respectfully, but then said, "Hearing you say that, I feel more strongly than ever that Annie *has* to go ahead and let Sam do this. You have to give your children their freedom, even if you do so with tremendous anxiety."

"No," said the wife. "This is a bad idea. He is too small. Don't do it." The husband responded, the wife responded to his response, I turned my head from side to side as each spoke as if I were watching a tennis match. My vision began to blur, and as they discussed my case with each other, I spaced out for a minute. A memory came to me then, of our pastor Veronica telling us just the week before how she gets direction from God in prayer; she said that when she prays for direction, one spot of illumination always appears just beyond her feet, a circle of light into which she can step. She moved away from the pulpit to demonstrate, stepping forward shyly—this big-boned African-American woman tramping like Charlie Chaplin into an imagined spotlight, and then, after standing there looking puzzled, she moved another step forward to where the light had gone, two feet ahead of where she had been standing, and then again. "We in our faith work," she said, stumble along toward where we think we're supposed to go, bumbling along, and here is what's so amazing—we end up getting exactly where we're supposed to be."

But I couldn't discern even what direction to face. And I didn't understand why as usual God couldn't give me a loud or obvious answer, through a megaphone or thunder, skywriting or stigmata. Why does God always use dreams, intuition, memory, phone calls, vague stirrings in my heart? I would say that this *really* doesn't work for me at all. Except that it does.

While the Zen adventurer and his wife engaged in a heated discussion on vision versus the sense one was born with, I imagined Sam floating down through the sky like a great dandelion fluff, weightless as the breeze, a marionette-boy with silky dark blonde hair, suspended by cords to a great wing of silk. I wanted to give him that lightness, but in the next moment I imagined him falling out of the sky, imagined the earth racing toward him. Oh, God, I said, inhaling loudly, tell me what to do—would it be so much skin off your nose just to give me a sign?

And then the music began.

Mandolin music. A folksy bluegrass trio began playing, the mandolin offering the quavering melody, then two guitars joined in, and then three voices singing. We turned slowly to look at the musicians. A woman got up from her table and began to dance on the lawn between us and the stage, all by herself, and I thought to myself, I wish I were the kind of person who could dance in public, not caring what everyone thought. And I wanted to be this way so badly that after a minute I just got up, moved closer to the music, toward the one woman dancing, and slowly and very shyly and without enormous visible grace, began to move in time to the music. I figured that once I stepped forward into that spotlight, another would appear some-where near my feet, and if it didn't, at least I'd have had the chance to dance.

So I did, dancing with my eyes closed so as not to be dis-tracted. Nietzsche said that he could only believe in a God who would dance, and I feel the same way: not Jesus as John Travolta but Jesus as Judith Jamison, the great black dancer with Alvin Ailey, a shining, long-limbed, elegant crane.

Then out of nowhere a memory bobbed into my head of the most important conversation I have ever had, and I understood that this was the next circle of light into which I might step. Many years ago, I was walking beside the salt marsh with a minister I had met recently. I was two months pregnant and had scheduled an abortion because I was alone and so broke. But I was having second thoughts. I decided to let this minister in on this, and after listening quietly, he said he thought I should have the abortion; he pointed out that there was no safety net underneath me at the time—no family money, no expected windfall—that there was nothing between me and the streets or welfare.

But what about God? I asked. What about faith?

Well, yes, the priest conceded, there's that. "But I'd like you to try something," he said. "Get quiet for a moment, and then think about having the abortion: if you feel a deep and secret sense of relief, pay attention to that. But if you feel deeply grieved at the thought of it, *listen* to that."

I did what he said, thought about the abortion, which theoretically and politically I support. But I was stabbed with grief, and the grief did not pass, and I canceled the abortion. And seven months later I gave birth to the little kid who now wanted to fly off the mountain.

So right then on the dance floor, dancing to the blue-grass music, I got very quiet. I thought about how I would feel if I let Sam jump: my heart leapt into my throat, as if to escape rising water. Then I thought about how I would feel if I called the paraglide pilot and canceled. I felt euphoric, like Zorba the Greek; I felt like getting everyone up on their feet so we could all dance the mazurka and clink steins full of root beer. Instead I went off to find a telephone, and cancel.

I really want my son to fly very high—in maybe ten years. But this time he wasn't going to get to hang in the air like a baby eagle.

He was a pretty good sport about it, though. He rolled his eyes at my conservative little decision, and crossed his arms, and growled, digging his heels in the dirt—it all lasted less than two minutes, and then he was done. I think he was secretly relieved. That night in the shadow of the mountain he would not be jumping off, we asked God to help us come up with a really exciting and safe way for Sam to celebrate his birthday. I felt the weight of the world lift off me. The moon rose so full and burned so yellow that night that it colored the sky green between itself and the snow-capped mountains.

The next day, out of the blue, a friend of ours called and asked Sam if he wanted to go inner-tubing, floating down a sleepy little creek at the foot of the mountain. Sleepy little creek I can do.

This is not to say that I didn't worry the rest of the afternoon about Sam drowning, or bashing his head against a rock in the stream, or being bitten by displaced water moccasins. But I only worried a little, and he had a fantastic day. Later, after dinner, after all the people from the conference sang him happy birthday and he'd opened all his presents, Sam and I stood outside in the moonlight that had turned the sky so green the night before. I no longer saw the mountain's muscles. I saw instead how lovely it was, delicate and feminine as Fuji. I did not know what any of this meant, only that I had asked for help and received it. Now I could say to God, Thank you for showing me I didn't have to toss my child off the mountain, and to my son, "Happy birthday, big boy, baby eagle, Sam," and he tucked his head in against his shoulder, closed his eyes, and smiled.

# Part Two

# CHURCH, PEOPLE, STEEPLE

*Late Fragment*

And did you get what
you wanted from this life even so?
I did.
And what did you want?
To call myself beloved, to feel myself
beloved on the earth.

RAYMOND CARVER

# ASHES

A sh Wednesday came early this year. It is supposed to be about preparation, about consecration, about moving toward Easter, toward resurrection and renewal. It offers us a chance to break through the distractions that keep us from living the basic Easter message of love, of living in wonder rather than doubt. For some people, it is about fasting, to symbolize both solidarity with the hungry and the hunger for God. (I, on the other hand, am not heavily into fasting; the thought of missing even a single meal sends me running in search of Ben and Jerry's Mint Oreo.)

So there are many ways to honor the day, but as far as I know, there is nothing in Scripture or tradition setting it aside as the day on which to attack one's child and then to flagellate oneself while the child climbs a tree and shouts down that he can't decide whether to hang himself or jump, even after it is pointed out nicely that he is only five feet from the ground.

But I guess every family celebrates in its own unique way.

Let me start over. You see, I tried at breakfast to get Sam interested in Ash Wednesday. I made him cocoa and gave a rousing talk on what it all means. We daub our foreheads with ashes, I explained, because they remind us of how much we miss and celebrate those who have already died. The ashes remind us of the finality of death. Like the theologian said, death is God's no to all human presumption. We are sometimes like the characters in *Waiting for Godot,* where the only visible redemption is the eventual appearance in Act Two of four or five new leaves on the pitiful tree. On such a stage, how can we cooperate with grace? How can we open ourselves up to it? How can we make room for anything new? How can we till the field? And so people also mark themselves with ashes to show that they trust in the alchemy God can work with those ashes—jogging us awake, moving us toward greater attention and openness and love.

Sam listened very politely to my little talk. Then when he thought I wasn't looking, he turned on the TV. I made him turn it off. I explained that in honor of Ash Wednesday we were not watching cartoons that morning. I told him he could draw if he wanted, or play with Legos. I got myself a cup of coffee and started looking at a book of photographs that someone had sent. One in particular caught my eye immediately. It was of a large Mennonite family, shot in black and white—a husband and wife and their fifteen children gathered around a highly polished oval table, their faces clearly, eerily reflected by the burnished wood. They looked surreal and serious; you saw in those long grave faces the echoes of the Last Supper. I wanted to show the photograph to Sam. But abruptly, hideously, Alvin and the Chipmunks were singing "Achy Breaky Heart" in their nasal demon-field way—on the TV that Sam had turned on again.

And I just lost my mind. I thought I might begin smashing things. Including Sam. I shouted at the top of my lungs, and I used the word *fucking,* as in "goddamn fucking TV that we're getting rid of," and I grabbed him by his pipe-cleaner arm and jerked him in the direction of his room, where he spent the next ten minutes crying bitter tears.

It's so awful, attacking your child. It is the worst thing I know, to shout loudly at this fifty-pound being with his huge trusting brown eyes. It's like bitch-slapping E. T.

I did what all good parents do: calmed down enough to go apologize, and beg for his forgiveness while simultaneously expressing a deep concern about his disappointing character. He said I was the meanest person on earth next to Darth Vader. We talked and then he went off to his room. I chastised myself silently while washing breakfast dishes, but then it was time for school and I couldn't find him anywhere. I looked everywhere in the house, in closets, under beds, and finally I heard him shouting from the branches of our tree.

I coaxed him down, dropped him off at school and felt terrible all day. Everywhere I went I'd see businessmen and women marching purposefully by with holy ashes on their foreheads. I couldn't go to church until that night to get my own little ash tilak, the reminder that I was forgiven. I thought about taking Sam out of school so that I could apologize some more. But I knew just enough to keep my mitts off him. Now, at seven, he is separating from me like mad and has made it clear that I need to give him a little bit more room. I'm not even allowed to tell him I love him these days. He is quite firm on this. "You tell me you love me all the time," he explained recently, "and I don't want you to anymore."

"At all?" I said.

"I just want you to tell me that you like me."

I said I would really try. That night, when I was tucking him in, I said, "Good night, honey. I really like you a lot."

There was silence in the dark. Then he said, "I like you too, Mom."

So I didn't take him out of school. I went for several walks, and I thought about ashes. I was sad that I am an awful person, that I am the world's meanest mother. I got sadder. And I got to thinking about the ashes of the dead.

Twice I have held the ashes of people I adored—my dad's, my friend Pammy's. Nearly twenty years ago I poured my father's into the water near Angel Island, late at night, but I was twenty-five years old and very drunk at the time and so my grief was anesthetized. When I opened the box of his ashes, I thought they would be nice and soft and, well, ashy, like the ones with which they anoint your forehead on Ash Wednesday. But they're the grittiest of elements, like not very good landscaping pebbles. As if they're made of bones or something.

I tossed a handful of Pammy's into the water way out past the Golden Gate Bridge during the day, with her husband and family, when I had been sober several years. And this time I was able to see, because it was daytime and I was sober, the deeply contradictory nature of ashes—that they are both so heavy and so light. They're impossible to let go of entirely. They stick to things, to your fingers, your sweater. I licked my friend's ashes off my hand, to taste them, to taste her, to taste what was left after all that was clean and alive had been consumed, burned away. They tasted metallic, and they blew every which way. We tried to strew them off the side of the boat romantically, with seals barking from the rocks on shore, under a true-blue sky, but they would not cooperate. They rarely will. It's frustrating if you are hoping to have a happy ending, or at least a little closure, a movie moment when you toss them into the air and they flutter and disperse. They don't. They cling, they haunt. They get in your hair, in your eyes, in your clothes.

By the time I reached into the box of Pammy's ashes, I had had Sam, so I was able to tolerate a bit more mystery and lack of order. That's one of the gifts kids give you, because after you have a child, things come out much less orderly and rational than they did before. It's so utterly bizarre to stare into the face of one of these tiny perfect beings and to understand that you (or someone a lot like you) grew them after a sweaty little bout of sex. And then, weighing in at the approximate poundage of a medium honeydew melon, they proceed to wedge open your heart. (Also, they help you see that you are as mad as a hatter, capable of violence just because Alvin and the Chipmunks are singing when you are trying to have a nice spiritual moment thinking about ashes.) By the time I held Pammy's ashes in my hand, I almost liked that they grounded me in all the sadness and mysteriousness; I could find a comfort in that. There's a kind of sweetness and attention that you can finally pay to the tiniest grains of life after you've run your hands through the ashes of someone you loved. Pammy's ashes clung to us. And so I licked them off my fingers. She was the most robust and luscious person I have ever known.

Sam went home after school with a friend, so I only saw him for a few minutes later, before he went off to dinner with his Big Brother Brian, as he does every Wednesday. I went to my church. The best part of the service was that we sang old hymns a cappella. There were only eight of us, mostly women, some black, some white, mostly well over fifty, scarves in their hair, lipstick, faces like pansies and cats. One of the older women was in a bad mood. I found this very scary, as if I were a flight attendant with one distressed passenger who wouldn't let me help. I tried to noodge her into a better mood with flattery and a barrage of questions about her job, garden, and dog, but she was having none of it.

This was discouraging at first, until I remembered another woman at our church, very old, from the South, tiny and black, who dressed in ersatz Coco Chanel outfits, polyester sweater sets, Dacron pillbox hats. They must have come from Mervyn's and Montgomery Ward because she didn't have any money. She was always cheerful—until she turned eighty and started going blind. She had a great deal of religious faith, and everyone assumed that she would adjust and find meaning in her loss—meaning and then acceptance and then joy—and we all wanted this because, let's face it, it's so inspiring and such a relief when people find a way to bear the unbearable, when you can organize things in such a way that a tiny miracle appears to have taken place and that love has once again turned out to be bigger than fear and death and blindness. But this woman would have none of it. She went into a deep depression and eventually left the church. The elders took communion to her in the afternoon on the first Sunday of the month—homemade bread and grape juice for the sacrament, and some bread to toast later—but she wouldn't be part of our community anymore. It must have been too annoying for everyone to be trying to manipulate her into being a better sport than she was capable of being. I always thought that was heroic of her, that it spoke of such integrity to refuse to pretend that you're doing well just to help other people deal with the fact that sometimes we face an impossible loss.

Still, on Ash Wednesday I sang, of faith and love, of repentance. We tore cloth rags in half to symbolize our repentance, our willingness to tear up the old pattern and await the new; we dipped our own fingers in ash and daubed it on our foreheads. I prayed for the stamina to bear mystery and stillness. I prayed for Sam to be able to trust me and for me to be able to trust me again, too.

When I got home, Sam was already asleep. Brian had put him to bed. I wanted to wake him up and tell him that it was OK that he wouldn't be who I tried to get him to be, that it was OK that he didn't cooperate with me all the time—that ashes don't, old people don't, why should little boys? But I let him alone. He was in my bed when I woke up the next morning, way over on the far left, flat and still as a shaft of light. I watched him sleep. His mouth was open. Just the last few weeks, he had grown two huge front teeth, big and white as Chiclets. He was snoring loudly for such a small boy.

I thought again about that photo of the Mennonites. In the faces of those fifteen children, reflected on their dining room table, you could see the fragile ferocity of their bond: it looked like a big wind could come and blow away this field of people on the shiny polished table. And the light shining around them where they stood was so evanescent that you felt that if the reflections were to go, the children would be gone, too.

More than anything else on earth, I do not want Sam ever to blow away, but you know what? He will. His ashes will stick to the fingers of someone who loves him. Maybe his ashes will blow that person into a place where things do not come out right, where things cannot be boxed up or spackled back together but where somehow he or she can see, with whatever joy can be mustered, the four or five leaves on the formerly barren tree.

"Mom?" he called out suddenly in his sleep.

"Yes," I whispered, "here I am," and he slung his arm toward the sound of my voice, out across my shoulders.

# WHY I MAKE SAM
# GO TO CHURCH

---

S am is the only kid he knows who goes to church—who
is made to go to church two or three times a month.
He rarely wants to. This is not exactly true: the truth is he
*never* wants to go. What young boy would rather be in
church on the weekends than hanging out with a friend? It
does not help him to be reminded that once he's there he
enjoys himself, that he gets to spend the time drawing in
the little room outside the sanctuary, that he only actually
has to sit still and listen during the short children's sermon.
It does not help that I always pack some snacks, some
Legos, his art supplies, and bring along any friend of his
whom we can lure into our churchy web. It does not help
that he genuinely cares for the people there. All that mat-
ters to him is that he alone among his colleagues is forced
to spend Sunday morning in church.

You might think, noting the bitterness, the resignation,
that he was being made to sit through a six-hour Latin
mass. Or you might wonder why I make this strapping,
exuberant boy come with me most weeks, and if you were
to ask, this is what I would say.

I make him because I can. I outweigh him by nearly seventy-five pounds.

But that is only part of it. The main reason is that I want to give him what I found in the world, which is to say a path and a little light to see by. Most of the people I know who have what I want—which is to say, purpose, heart, balance, gratitude, joy—are people with a deep sense of spirituality. They are people in community, who pray, or practice their faith; they are Buddhists, Jews, Christians—people banding together to work on themselves and for human rights. They follow a brighter light than the glimmer of their own candle; they are part of something beautiful. I saw something once from the Jewish Theological Seminary that said, "A human life is like a single letter of the alphabet. It can be meaningless. Or it can be a part of a great meaning." Our funky little church is filled with people who are working for peace and freedom, who are out there on the streets and inside praying, and they are home writing letters, and they are at the shelters with giant platters of food.

When I was at the end of my rope, the people at St. Andrew tied a knot in it for me and helped me hold on. The church became my home in the old meaning of *home*—that it's where, when you show up, they have to let you in. They let me in. They even said, "You come back now."

My relatives all live in the Bay Area and I adore them, but they are all as skittishly self-obsessed as I am, which I certainly mean in the nicest possible way. Let's just say that I do not leave family gatherings with the feeling that I have just received some kind of spiritual chemotherapy. But I do when I leave St. Andrew.

"Let's go, baby," I say cheerfully to Sam when it is time to leave for church, and he looks up at me like a puppy eyeing the vet who is standing there with the needle.

Sam was welcomed and prayed for at St. Andrew seven months before he was born. When I announced during worship that I was pregnant, people cheered. All these old people, raised in Bible-thumping homes in the Deep South, clapped. Even the women whose grown-up boys had been or were doing time in jails or prisons rejoiced for me. And then almost immediately they set about providing for us. They brought clothes, they brought me casseroles to keep in the freezer, they brought me assurance that this baby was going to be a part of the family. And they began slipping me money.

Now, a number of the older black women live pretty close to the bone financially on small Social Security checks. But routinely they sidled up to me and stuffed bills in my pocket—tens and twenties. It was always done so stealthily that you might have thought they were slipping me bindles of cocaine. One of the most consistent donors was a very old woman named Mary Williams, who is in her mid-eighties now, so beautiful with her crushed hats and hallelujahs; she always brought me plastic Baggies full of dimes, noosed with little wire twists.

I was usually filled with a sense of something like shame until I'd remember that wonderful line of Blake's—that we are here to learn to endure the beams of love—and I would take a long deep breath and force these words out of my strangulated throat: "Thank you."

I first brought Sam to church when he was five days old. The women there very politely pretended to care how I was doing but were mostly killing time until it was their turn to hold Sam again. They called him "our baby" or sometimes "my baby." "Bring me my baby!" they'd insist. "Bring me that baby now!" "Hey, you're hogging that baby."

I believe that they came to see me as Sam's driver, hired to bring him and his gear back to them every Sunday.

Mary Williams always sits in the very back by the door. She is one of those unusually beautiful women—beautiful like a river. She has dark skin, a long broad nose, sweet full lips, and what the theologian Howard Thurman calls "quiet eyes." She raised five children as a single mother, but one of her boys drowned when he was young, and she has the softness and generosity and toughness of someone who has endured great loss. During the service she praises God in a nonstop burble, a glistening dark brook. She says, "Oh, yes. . . . Uh-huh. . . . My sweet Lord. Thank you, thank you."

Sam loves her, and she loves him, and she still brings us Baggies full of dimes even though I'm doing so much better now. Every Sunday I nudge Sam in her direction, and he walks to where she is sitting and hugs her. She smells him behind his ears, where he most smells like sweet unwashed new potatoes. This is in fact what I think God may smell like, a young child's slightly dirty neck. Then Sam leaves the sanctuary and returns to his drawings, his monsters, dinosaurs, birds. I watch Mary Williams pray sometimes. She clutches her hands together tightly and closes her eyes most of the way so that she looks blind; because she is so unself-conscious, you get to see someone in a deeply interior pose. You get to see all that intimate resting. She looks as if she's holding the whole earth together, or making the biggest wish in the world. Oh, yes, Lord. Uh-huh.

It's funny: I always imagined when I was a kid that adults had some kind of inner toolbox, full of shiny tools: the saw of discernment, the hammer of wisdom, the sandpaper of patience. But then when I grew up I found that life handed you these rusty bent old tools—friendships, prayer, conscience, honesty—and said, Do the best you can with these, they will have to do. And mostly, against all odds, they're enough.

Not long ago I was driving Sam and his friend Josh over to Josh's house where the boys were going to spend the night. But out of the blue, Josh changed his mind about wanting Sam to stay over. "I'm tired," he said suddenly, "and I want to have a quiet night with my mom." Sam's face went white and blank; he has so little armor. He started crying. I tried to manipulate Josh into changing his mind, and I even sort of vaguely threatened him, hinting that Sam or I might cancel a date with *him* sometime, but he stayed firm. After a while Sam said he wished we'd all get hit by a car, and Josh stared out the window nonchalantly. I thought he might be about to start humming. It was one of those times when you wish you were armed so you could attack the kid who has hurt your own child's feelings.

"Sam?" I asked. "Can I help in any way? Shall we pray?"

"I just wish I'd never been born."

But after a moment, he said yes, I should pray. To myself.

So I prayed that God would help me figure out how to stop living in the problem and to move into the solution.

That was all. We drove along for a while. I waited for a sign of improvement. Sam said, "I guess Josh wishes I had never been born."

Josh stared out the window: dum de dum.

I kept asking God for help, and after a while I realized something—that Josh was not enjoying this either. He was just trying to take care of himself, and I made the radical decision to let him off the hook. I imagined gently lifting him off the hook of my judgment and setting him back on the ground.

And a moment later, he changed his mind. Now, maybe this was the result of prayer, or forgiveness; maybe it was a coincidence. I will never know. But even before Josh changed his mind, I did know one thing for sure, and this was that Sam and I would be going to church the next morning. Mary Williams would be sitting in the back near the door, in a crumpled hat. Sam would hug her; she would close her eyes and smell the soft skin of his neck, just below his ears.

What I didn't know was that Josh would want to come with us too. I didn't know that when I stopped by his house to pick up Sam the next morning, he would eagerly run out ahead of Sam to ask if he could come. And another thing I didn't know was that Mary Williams was going to bring us another bag of dimes. It had been a little while since her last dime drop, but just when I think we've all grown out of the ritual, she brings us another stash. Mostly I give them to street people. Some sit like tchotchkes on bookshelves around the house. Mary doesn't know that professionally I'm doing much better now; she doesn't know that I no longer really need people to slip me money. But what's so dazzling to me, what's so painful and poignant, is that she doesn't bother with what I think she knows or doesn't know about my financial life. She just knows we need another bag of dimes, and that is why I make Sam go to church.

# TRAVELING MERCIES

Broken things have been on my mind lately because so much has broken in my life this year and in the lives of the people I love—hearts, health, confidence. Our wonderful friend Ken Nelson died of AIDS just the other day, and that was terribly painful. Then not long after, my old friend Mimi, the mother of my junior doubles partner Bee, began to die after a long struggle with a rare blood disease.

Our preacher Veronica said recently that this is life's nature: that lives and hearts get broken—those of people we love, those of people we'll never meet. She said that the world sometimes feels like the waiting room of the emergency ward and that we who are more or less OK for now need to take the tenderest possible care of the more wounded people in the waiting room, until the healer comes. You sit with people, she said, you bring them juice and graham crackers.

And then she went on vacation.

"Traveling mercies," the old people at our church said to her when she left. This is what they always say when one of us goes off for a while. Traveling mercies: love the journey, God is with you, come home safe and sound.

Besides the big brokennesses, I've noticed all sorts of really dumb things breaking lately, too. I've had a dozen calls from friends reporting broken cars, water heaters, a window, even a finger. So I've been on the lookout for something wonderful to happen, because of this story I heard recently: Carolyn Myss, the medical intuitive who writes and lectures about why people don't heal, flew to Russia a few years ago to give some lectures. Everything that could go wrong did—flights were canceled or overbooked, connections missed, her reserved room at the hotel given to someone else. She kept trying to be a good sport, but finally, two mornings later, on the train to her conference on healing, she began to whine at the man sitting beside her about how infuriating her journey had been thus far.

It turned out that this man worked for the Dalai Lama. And he said—gently—that they believe when a lot of things start going wrong all at once, it is to protect something big and lovely that is trying to get itself born—and that this something needs for you to be distracted so that it can be born as perfectly as possible.

I believe this to be true. And I especially believe it when other people's things are breaking down. When it's my stuff, I believe the direct cause is my bad character. For instance, not long ago a car I was leasing broke down irretrievably, and while trying to find a secondhand car, I rented a car which broke down two days later. I did not find this very inspiring: I did not look around to see what lovely thing was trying to get itself born. I was just deeply disturbed. Still, I was being a pretty good sport until out of nowhere it began to rain. And it rained, and rained.

I'm not sure why, looking back at all those broken cars with the rain pouring down, it seemed like a good idea to buy a convertible. Maybe it was because so many things had gone so badly or been so troubling this year that I just wanted to feel lighter, or have a little fun or fresh air.

But in any case, I bought an old Volkswagen convertible. I've always loved Volkswagens. They're cheap and they run forever. And I wanted something reliable that didn't waste gas, something funky and smart, a little rusty, a little banged up, like me.

I didn't set out to get a convertible; I started by thinking seriously about Jettas, because they're sporty but in a touching, hippie way, like Pete Seeger wearing new Reeboks. Then, on the day the rains began, I heard about a '92 Cabriolet, which is the convertible form of the Jetta. This one had low mileage, as well as five speeds, and white fake-leather seats. It was teal green, and cheap. I called the owner, who was an Iranian woman.

She and I took the car for a ride, and it drove like a dream. I took it in to a Volkswagen diagnostician, who said it was a terrific car.

So I bought it.

And the rains poured down.

Sam loved the car. We tooled all over town in it, listening to oldies on the radio. I decided to buy brand-new tires in deference to the bad weather; the front wheels needed realigning anyway. So I took it to a tire shop in Marin where there are always a million new tires stacked in front. I bought four tires, arranged for the realignment and a few miscellaneous repairs, and bonded like mad with the woman behind the counter. Her name was Matty. She was my new best friend.

I picked up my car that night and said good-bye to my new best friend. "Come back in forty thousand miles, and we'll cut you another great deal," said my new best friend's dad. He looked like an old golf pro in a 49ers jacket.

Two days and forty miles later, on a Saturday afternoon, Sam and I were on our way out of town. We were going to say good-bye to Mimi, who lived and was dying half an hour away. But all of a sudden, at the stop sign of a busy intersection, there was a sound from the front of the car. It was a bad sound, a slippery crashing, as if the car had prolapse, as if all of its internal organs were trying to fall out of its vagina. The car wouldn't go forward. Sam and I gaped at each other. I tried to ease the car into first, but it made the bad sound again and would not move. Cars behind me started to honk. "Move your fucking car," someone shouted. Everyone started honking. It was my own private New York City.

It would be hard to capture how I felt at that moment. It was a nightmare: Bad Mind kicked in. Bad Mind can't wait for this kind of opportunity: "I told you so," Bad Mind says. It whispers to me that I am doomed because I am such a loser. And Bad Mind can lean ever so slightly toward paranoia. "The woman you bought this car from," it whispered, "is already on a plane back to Iran, celebrating." Horns blared, metal ground against metal under my hood. "I'm freaking out," I said to Sam. I turned on my hazard lights and did Lamaze. The rain poured down.

"Move the goddamn fucking car," someone shouted.

I tried to call AAA on my cheap lousy car phone but it wasn't working. I tried to get the car into gear; it brayed, and I started to cry. I cried because Mimi was dying, and because Bad Mind was saying she would die before we had a chance to say good-bye, and because nothing worked at all anymore, not the whole world, not relationships, not even my new goddamn car.

"Will you pray with me?" I asked Sam. He appeared to be listening to something in the distance or trying to remember someone's name. Car horns continued to honk while he considered my request. "OK," he said, "but wait a minute." Then he stuck his head out the window, and screwing up his face, wild and flushed, he shouted, "Stop yelling at us, you fucking assholes!"

We said a prayer together that we find a solution, that we feel calmer. I don't believe in God as an old man in the clouds—"bespectacled old Yahweh," as the late great John Gardner put it, "scratching his chin through his mountains of beard." But I do believe that God is with us even when we're at our craziest and that this goodness guides, provides, protects, even in traffic.

A few minutes later, a man bent down to peer in the window. "Do you need a hand?" I nodded. "OK," he said. "You steer. I'll push."

He pushed us out of the traffic and over to the sidewalk.

When we were out of the road and the man had left, I looked at Sam for a while. "Now what?" he said. I sighed, not knowing what to do next. Then, on the screen of my mind, Matty's face appeared. Matty, my new best friend, and all those tires.

"I know where to go!" I said. "To the tire shop!"

Sam thought about this with a dubious expression on his face, but then shrugged. "OK," he said, and we ran there in the rain. Matty wasn't in, but her father was.

"My car broke down six blocks away," I said, out of breath.

"Listen," he said nicely, "we're a tire shop."

"But you fixed non-tire things on Thursday, too."

Sam peered at me with the same mix of faith and worry that I felt. Finally, I said to the man, "I'm not trying to con you into helping us. All I know is that we were supposed to come here. That if we came here, we would be helped."

He hemmed and hawed, and then sighed deeply. "Well," he said finally, "there's this Mexican guy in the back."

My soul heaved a huge sigh of relief. Of *course* there's a Mexican man in the back, I thought. He was our *connection*.

"I suppose I could get him," said Matty's father. I smiled.

Joaquim came out a few minutes later, tall and beautiful in greasy coveralls. We explained our problem and that we knew he just worked on tires, but we still needed help. "OK," he said. We piled into his broken-down old car and drove to mine. Joaquim opened the hood, looked in, then peered underneath the car. "Ohhh," he said.

"What should we do?" I asked.

"We need to go get Al," he said.

Oh, I thought, of course. Of course we need to go get Al.

I hadn't a clue who Al was until we drove back and picked him up. Al was very small and did not seem to speak any English at all. He drove us all in a rusty truck back to my car, and then found a pitiful short piece of fraying rope in his glove box. It was like girl rope, like a bit of string I might have in my purse, that you couldn't do anything with except maybe tie up your hair. Joaquim used it to tie my Volkswagen to Al's crummy truck. It had stopped raining.

Joaquim and Sam got into the VW; Al and I started towing them. Smash crash, it was like the demolition derby. We lurched and crashed along until finally we nosed right into the greasy work deck of the tire shop.

The next thing I knew my car was on the lift and in the air. Joaquim and Al peered up into its innards with flashlights, consulting in hushed tones like doctors. In due time Joaquim came over to talk to me gravely, as though I were the next of kin.

"It was a loose bolt," he said. "It's going to take me at least fifteen minutes to fix."

We called Bee and said we would be on our way soon, but she said maybe we should come the next day, when her mother might have more energy. So Sam and I went to a parking lot nearby and played soccer with an old tennis ball that was losing its nap.

It all made me think of Eugene O'Neill's line, "Man is born broken. He lives by mending. The grace of God is glue."

When we went back to the tire shop, Matty's father gave us a bill for thirty-six dollars, but I slipped Joaquim and Al each a twenty.

We drove on home. Back in the saddle again, I thought to myself, the story of my life. I still did not know what was trying to distract me so it could get itself born, but I felt happier than I had in a long time.

The next morning Sam woke up with a cold, so we *still* couldn't go visit Bee and Mimi. Finally, several days later, with Sam back in school, I went to visit them by myself.

I walked into their house at nine, into this wooden palace as familiar to me as my own childhood home, the walls covered with framed photos I've been looking at for thirty-some years, Mimi's tiny framed oil paintings of flowers hung all over the house like flat bouquets. Outside the windows were trees and roses, the eastern shores of San Francisco Bay, blue waters, blue sky: birds, life, motion, stillness. Bee's eyes were red from crying, the brown irises clouded with sun damage from our tennis years. We walked hand in hand down the hallway to where Mimi lay asleep on her bed, breathing in the loud labored way that means the end is near. Bee and I talked for a moment, and then she sat in the chair beside the big bed, holding her mother's hand, and I lay down beside Mimi, because she was the most gregarious woman I've ever known, flamboyant and loving as the Broadway stars she loved, and she seemed a little lonely. Bee held Mimi's hand to her face and her chest; I stroked Mimi's shoulders and smoothed her hair. We talked to her the way you talk to a sleepy child too troubled to fall asleep. We whispered that we loved her. We told her over and over that we would stay with her as long as she needed but that when she was ready, we were also willing to let her go. And that she was safe, with God here now on this side, and in a moment with God on the other. Traveling mercies, I whispered into her ear. We said prayers softly, although Bee is not particularly religious, and we lit candles, and held Mimi lightly so she could take off when she was ready. The space between each new breath became longer and longer, until an hour later there was all space, and she died.

Now. Maybe you think it is arrogant or self-centered or ridiculous for me to believe that God bothered to wiggle a cheap bolt out of my new used car because he or she needed to keep me away for a few days until just the moment when my old friend most needed me to help her mother move into whatever comes next. Maybe nothing conscious helped to stall me so that I would be there when I could be most useful. Or maybe it did. I'll never know for sure. And anyway, it doesn't really matter. It was just such a blessing to have been there helping Bee bathe her mother's body with beautiful soaps, smooth her skin with lotion, working as thoroughly and gently as Mimi must have done forty-three years ago, when Bee had just been born.

*Part Three*

---

# TRIBE

All actual life is encounter.

MARTIN BUBER

# FIELDS

---

I was remembering an old story the other day about a man getting drunk at a bar in Alaska. He's telling the bartender how he recently lost whatever faith he'd had after his twin-engine plane crashed in the tundra.

"Yeah," he says bitterly. "I lay there in the wreckage, hour after hour, nearly frozen to death, crying out for God to save me, praying for help with every ounce of my being, but he didn't raise a finger to help. So I'm done with that whole charade."

"But," said the bartender, squinting an eye at him, "you're here. You *were* saved."

"Yeah, that's right," says the man. "Because finally some goddamn *Eskimo* came along . . ."

I'd been sick for a while recently with all the colds and infirmities that were going around the Bay Area—colds, flus, general malaise. In the brief periods when I didn't have some horrible bug, Sam was home sick from school, bleary, feverish, needy. We seemed to be catching everything from the virulent little children at Sam's school, and I had considered buying us both biohazard gear. But a brief period of good health followed, leading me to believe that the worst was over. And then a few days ago, I woke up with a flu whose main symptom was a splitting headache.

It was so sunny out that morning when I went down to retrieve my newspaper that I shrank back from the glow, squinting like a mole. I need help, I said to God. And about a moment later, Rick Fields drove by on his way home.

Rick is the editor in chief of *Yoga Journal.* He moved in with his girlfriend at the far end of our street a few years ago, and then about ten minutes later he was diagnosed with lung cancer. It had metastasized to his brain. He has done surgery, chemo, radiation, and every imaginable alternative medicine but is still living with both his beautiful girlfriend and stage-four metastatic lung cancer. He usually drives by our house a couple of times a day and seems to be in a quietly good mood most of the time.

I just do not understand this conceptually.

Several weeks before this latest flu, when I had a simple head cold, I pounded on his windshield when he attempted to drive by and said, "Why are you doing this to me? Look at me—I'm *congested.*" He smiled. He loves me, loves my emotional drag-queeny self. He's ten years older than I, and he looks a little bit like Stephen Spielberg, especially because he wears a baseball cap most of the time now and does not shave every day.

He stops by sometimes with little animals for Sam—a rubber gecko, a windup ladybug, a clay turtle.

I read an interview he did for a Buddhist quarterly recently, in which he said that he's so savoring the moments of his life right now, so acutely aware of love and small pleasures that he no longer feels that he has a life-threatening disease: he now says he's leading a disease-threatening life.

When I saw him the morning I had the headache and flu, he looked grizzled and radiant. He didn't see me for a moment; he had his window open and his nose in the air, was obviously sniffing the breeze, while I stood there gripping my lower back like Grandpa Walton.

"Hey, you," he said, great sweetness rendered in a low and gravelly voice.

"Oh, Rick," I groaned. "I have a terrible headache. And I have *body* aches, and I want to hang myself. And here you're such a good sport even though you have all these *tumors.*"

"Sometimes colds and flus are harder to handle than cancer." He smiled. He has a handsome turtlish look about him. He's a squintier since he got sick, more leathery. He wears worn jeans, old T-shirts usually in some shade of blue and bearing the emblematic symbols of various gatherings and causes. This particular day he wore a sky-blue shirt from a gathering called "Arizona Tibet" and a black baseball cap from a big powwow in South Dakota. "Did you take some aspirin?" he asked. I nodded.

"You'll be better soon," he said kindly. "God, what a day!"

"Oh, *stop,*" I said.

In his interview in the Buddhist magazine, he'd said, "I'm going to live until I die. And the doctor is going to live until he dies. He thinks he knows when *I'm* going to die, but he doesn't even know when *he's* going to die."

"Can I do anything to help you today?" he asked.

"Are you going to work this morning?" He nodded. "Will you stop by and get Sam on your way to work, and then drop him off at school?" And he said that of course he would.

We made arrangements for Rick to come by in an hour, and I went back upstairs. I hate being the kind of person who tries to get someone with stage-four metastatic lung cancer to feel sorry for her just because she has a headache. (Though it *was* an ice-pick headache.) But the way I see things, God loves you the same whether you're being elegant or not. It feels much better when you are, but even when you can't fake it, God still listens to your prayers. And he or she will still try to send you an Eskimo

Again and again I tell God I need help, and God says, "Well, isn't that fabulous? Because I need help too. So you go get that old woman over there some water, and I'll figure out what we're going to do about *your* stuff." Maybe Rick had told God (as he understands God) that he needed some energy that morning, and God had said, "Well, great, because Sam Lamott needs a ride to school. Could you do that for me? And I'll be getting you some strength."

At any rate, Rick came by for Sam at nine, and they drove off happily together. I sat outside on the front step for a while. The aspirin had kicked in, and I was feeling better, though not well enough to work. But *Rick* is going to work, I'm sure one of my parents would have pointed out helpfully if they had been there. But they weren't, and I'm not Rick. So I decided to go to the beach at San Quentin, and practice living as if today was one of a precious few left to me. What a concept.

I had only driven twenty feet or so when a major problem arose.

Everything *smelled* too strong. Maybe it was because I was sick, but my car smelled of dog and an old school lunch on the floor of the backseat, and when I rolled down the window to air it all out, tar fumes poured in. As I drove along, I kept sniffing the air like a Doberman pinscher, until even the inside of my *nose* started to smell bad: it smelled like two tiny windowless hallways. I shook my head, realizing once again that I am not all there. I thought about Rick instead, about the notes that make up the major chord he plays these days. Compassion is one of them, of course, since he's a nice Buddhist boy. And being present, as in "You must be present to win." He said in the interview, "I'll live as well, as deeply, as madly as I can—until I die." And Rule Sixty-two, which says you should not take yourself too damn seriously. Rick exudes the good-humored dignity of someone living by Rule Sixty-two. So I decided to try and play this same chord, too, on my heart's twangy old banjo.

I stopped and bought the new *People* magazine and—talk about living deeply and madly—a can of real Coca-Cola. On my last day, I won't be drinking *Diet* Coke. If I am, shoot me.

I drove to San Quentin. I'm drawn to the beach there because my dad taught English at the prison when I was a kid, and I feel that there is still a little bit of him in the sand. He published a number of short stories during the sixties about teaching English to the prisoners, and these pieces were where he made a name for himself. He wrote a biography of the prison that came out when I was seven; then when I was a teenager, I got to stand outside late at night in vigils with him and his friends, protesting death penalties and inhumane conditions. I can remember exactly how he smelled—of chamois shirts, beer, cigarettes. He smelled like a tall male, and of hiking, and of books and blue jeans.

His friends would pass around flasks of whiskey, and because it was always late and cold, they would pass the flask to me. And I would have a sip with the men outside the walls of San Quentin. The moon would be out, and the stars.

San Quentin's is the safest beach in the world. We're not talking lifeguards here who might yell at someone who's being rude—we're talking armed guards, in watchtowers, two blocks away.

Beachwise, it's about as basic as it gets—the Platonic essence of beach. Sand, water, sky, eucalyptus trees jutting over the sand from the bordering hillside. There are no accommodations—no public bathrooms, no places to buy food. Compared to the grandeur of Marin County beaches like Stinson or Bolinas, it's not that great a beach; but sometimes the more luscious and robust a place is, the more you forget about the comfort of quiet, of slow.

Normally I like luscious. I like festive beach umbrellas and chaise longues. I like long white stretches of sand, and I am heavily into unguents. I like a lot of people around who have been paid to help me, and a small medical staff for any tropics-related incidents that may crop up, like blood blisters, say, or shark bite. Also, I like to nurse virgin blender drinks in which pineapple chunks bob on cocktail toothpicks with frilly plastic panties.

But I also happen to love the beach at San Quentin, which on this day struck me as being the Rick Fields of beaches: plain, beautiful, private. There was no one on the beach when I arrived, so I hummed my little chord and sat in the warm sand, reading my magazine. A small voice inside me whispered to look up, to be here now, and avoid the rush. I will, I whispered back, as soon as I finish this article.

After a while, though, I heard footsteps coming down the stairs to the beach, and I looked up. A huge man with an ice chest and a radio had arrived, wearing a tank top so that I could see what appeared to be the entire Book of Revelations tattooed on his arms. He nodded hello and walked over to the left, where he set up camp. He unfurled a beach towel and then turned on the radio to a talk show. I covered my face with my hands.

I want my beach back, I whispered. Gimme my beach back!

But no: instead there were more footsteps, and I turned to find a woman coming down the steps with a child of one or so in a backpack and a matching child in her arms. The one in her arms jabbed the one on her back, and both babies began to cry.

The mother walked over to the right and put the babies in the sand, where they lurched about like twenty-pound crack addicts. They shrieked with joy. My headache, which had been dozing, woke up and looked around. Shhhhhh, I whispered to it: listen! The man had turned off his radio.

I looked over at him gratefully, only to find that he'd taken off his tank top and fallen asleep on his back. He had a hairy stomach and big breasts. I wanted to go over and ask if he'd mind if I covered him up with my beach towel.

I took a long deep breath to calm myself: breathing in I calm myself, breathing out I smile. . . . I've been around, I know a Thich Nhat Hanh mantra or two. But after I had done this for a minute, I noticed a bad smell mingling with the scent of eucalyptus. It wafted over from the general direction of the driftwood that blankets the back part of the beach. But I couldn't put my finger on what the new smell was. It wasn't fishy or salty or sweet. It was something very familiar, very bodily, but not the usual suspects—not feet or crotch or armpits. It smelled like a wild animal who was letting itself go, but not like an animal who had died. I sniffed the air, trying to figure out what it was. It smelled like a bedridden person, like someone whose inside smells have inadvertently gotten out. It smelled like people in convalescent homes.

I watched the tide roll in and carpet the sand. The sleeping man slept and the babies played. My friend Pammy always had a strong earthy smell about her until she got sick, because she never wore deodorant. The sicker she got, the milder her smells grew. As she could do less and less in the world, she started to smell younger and soapier, as if she had peaked agewise at thirty-seven and was now in reverse, scrolling back toward the day she was born.

The smell on the beach grew stronger and stronger until I *finally* figured out what it reminded me of: the inside of belly buttons. It was the smell of a tiny bit of pflug that has snuggled way down deep inside a person, gotten a little wet, a little dirty. It's like a small practice burial site; it carries a hint of the grave. I was a teenager the first time I noticed it. Bee and I were trying to go to sleep in the guest room of her house when we discovered that if you rubbed your finger inside your belly button, your finger came out smelling terrible. This sent us into paroxysms of laughter, but after that night I couldn't stop doing it. It became a weird little compulsion for a while. It left me feeling deeply ashamed and scared, left me worrying that all the other girls in eighth grade had been dealing with this situation all along. As if everyone but Bee and I knew how to tend to this, and all your fresher women were using something sold in the back of magazines between the teeth whiteners and the canine itch-control products.

Talk about self-referential: knowing the smell inside your navel. Good Lord, if people in New York found out about this, you could never live it down. But as I have heard Rick quote several times, "Death is real, comes without warning; this body will be a corpse." So smelling these smells is to become friends with one part of ourselves. It's like the Rodgers and Hammerstein song "Getting to Know You."

The babies, rolling around in the sand, had begun to look like breaded veal cutlets. I smiled. Pammy had wanted to be a mother so badly; then she got cancer instead, and it looked like her dream was over. Throughout her chemotherapy, all of us were praying for a miracle, which was supposed to be a call from the doctor announcing that the cancer was gone and would never come back. But instead the adoption lawyer called to tell Pammy and her husband about a baby girl soon to be born near Sacramento, who would be needing a home.

I wanted to cry out, "No, Pammy, you mustn't do this—what if you get sick again?" But I didn't. God shut me up. And when Rebecca came to live with them, when she was three days old, she literally saved Pammy. She literally gave her life.

Both babies on the beach finally fell asleep. The mother sighed a grunty exhausted sigh and let her head drop down onto her chest. It had grown very quiet on the beach again, and I dug a fingernail into the palm of my hand, traced its furrows, the wrinkles, the life line. A breeze began to blow, finally blowing in the smells of the sea, of the sun on the salty water. I listened to the sound of the air moving softly and thought about my father at the gates of the prison, thirty years ago, standing with his friends and me underneath the moon. He was the same age when he died that Rick is now: fifty-six. The message on my father's answering machine always said, "The freedom train is coming!" The message on Rick's machine says, "The road to enlightenment is long and difficult, and you should try not to forget snacks and magazines." I felt a stab of sadness at the thought of Rick actually dying, at the thought of having to tell Sam, but I also thought how invaluable it is to know this man, this mensch who lives at the end of our street with his pow-wow caps and raspy voice, who sniffs the air as he drives off to work, who still stops to reach out to his crazy single-mother neighbor. And this thought made me so happy that I felt like going over to the man on the beach towel and giving him something, like a great rubber lizard or something. But of course, I had nothing like that to give him, and anyway, he was still asleep. So, feeling stiff and creaky, I got up and walked over to where the mother sat and gave her my *People* magazine. She was really surprised and pleased. She fished a green apple out of her diaper bag and gave it to me. We watched her babies sleep for a minute. I walked back to where I'd been sitting, polishing my apple on my T-shirt, just above my heart. Then I lifted the apple to my face, breathed in the sharp apple smell, and held it against my nose like an oxygen mask.

# FORGIVENESS

I went around saying for a long time that I am not one of those Christians who is heavily into forgiveness—that I am one of the other kind. But even though it was funny, and actually true, it started to be too painful to stay this way. They say we are not punished for the sin but by the sin, and I began to feel punished by my unwillingness to forgive. By the time I decided to become one of the ones who *is* heavily into forgiveness, it was like trying to become a marathon runner in middle age; everything inside me either recoiled, as from a hot flame, or laughed a little too hysterically. I tried to will myself into forgiving various people who had harmed me directly or indirectly over the years—four former Republican presidents, three relatives, two old boyfriends, and one teacher in a pear tree—it was "The Twelve Days of Christmas" meets *Taxi Driver*. But in the end I could only pretend that I had. I decided I was starting off with my sights aimed too high. As C. S. Lewis says in *Mere Christianity*, "If we really want to learn how to forgive, perhaps we had better start with something easier than the Gestapo."

So I decided to put everyone I'd ever lived with, slept with, or been reviewed by on hold, and to start with some-one I barely knew whom I had only hated for a while.

I'd had an enemy—an Enemy Lite—for some time, the parent of one of the children in Sam's first grade class, although she was so warm and friendly that it might have astounded her to learn that we were enemies. But I, the self-appointed ethical consultant for the school, can tell you that it's true. Somewhere in the back of my mind I knew she was divorced and maybe lonely, but she also had mean eyes. In the first weeks of first grade she looked at me like I was a Rastafarian draft-dodger type and then, over time, as if I were a dazed and confused alien space traveler. Now, I'll be the first to admit that I had a certain amount of trouble adjusting once Sam started first grade. I couldn't seem to get the hang of things; there was too much to remember, too much to do. But Sam's first grade teacher was so kind and forgiving that I just didn't trouble my pretty head about schedules, homework, spelling lists, and other sundry unpleasantries. Nor was I able to help out in the classroom much. There were all these mothers who were always cooking holiday theme-park treats for the class; they always drove the kids—including mine—on their field trips, and they also seemed to read all the papers the school sent home, which I think is actually a little show-offy. Also, it gave them an unfair advantage. They knew, for instance, from the first day of school that Wednesdays were minimum days, with school out over forty-five minutes earlier than usual, and they flaunted it, picking up their kids at just the right time, week after week.

I somehow managed to make it into October without figuring out this little scheduling quirk.

Finally, though, one Wednesday, I stopped by Sam's classroom and found him—once again—drawing with his teacher. The teacher said gently, "Annie? Did you not know that school gets out an hour early on Wednesdays?"

"Ah," I said.

"Didn't you get the papers the school mailed to you this summer?"

I racked my brain, and finally I did remember some papers coming in the mail from school. And I remembered really meaning to read them.

Sam sat there drawing with a grim autistic stare.

Well, my enemy found out.

She showed up two days later all bundled up in a down jacket, because it was cold and she was one of the parents who was driving the kids on their first field trip. Now, this was not a crime against nature or me in and of itself. The crime was that below the down jacket, she was wearing latex bicycle shorts. She wears latex bicycle shorts nearly every day, and I will tell you why: because she can. She weighs about eighty pounds. She has gone to the gym almost every day since her divorce, and she does not have an ounce of fat on her body. I completely hate that in a person. I consider it an act of aggression against the rest of us mothers who forgot to start working out after we had our kids.

Oh, and one more thing: she still had a Ronald Reagan bumper sticker on her white Volvo, seven years after he left office.

The day of the field trip, she said sweetly, "I just want you to know, Annie, that if you have any other questions about how the classroom works, I'd really love to be there for you."

I smiled back at her. I thought such awful thoughts that I cannot even say them out loud because they would make Jesus want to drink gin straight out of the cat dish.

It drove me to my knees. I prayed about it. I prayed because my son loves her son, and my son is so kind that it makes me want to be a better person, a person who does not hate someone just because she wears latex bicycle shorts. I prayed for a miracle; I wrote her name down on a slip of paper, folded it up, and put it in the box that I use as God's In box. "Help," I said to God.

There wasn't much noticeable progress for a while. On the last day of first grade, I was asked to bake something for the farewell party. I couldn't do it. I was behind in my work. Also, I was in a bad mood. But I at least *went* to the party, and I ate the delicious cookies my enemy made, and we mingled a little, and I thought that this was progress. Then she had to go and wreck everything by asking, "Did *you* bake anything?"

I don't bake. I baked for school once and it was a bad experience: Sam was in kindergarten at the little Christian school he attended, and I baked a dozen cupcakes for his class's Christmas party and set them out to cool. Sam and I went outside to sweep the Astroturf. (OK, OK, I also don't garden.) Suddenly Sadie came tearing outside—our dog who is so obedient and eager to please. But there was icing in the fur of her muzzle and a profoundly concerned look on her face. Oh, my God, she seemed to be saying with her eyes: Terrible news from the kitchen!

Sam looked at me with total disgust, like "You ignorant slut—you left the cupcakes out where the *dog* could get them."

The next morning I bought cupcakes at Safeway. Like I said: I don't bake.

I also don't push Sam to read. There wasn't much pressure for anyone to read in first grade, but by second grade, it was apparently critical to national security that your kid be reading. He brought home bulletins from time to time to this effect. My kid was not reading. I mean, per se.

My enemy's child was reading proficiently, like a little John Kenneth Galbraith in a Spiderman T-shirt. He is what is referred to as an "early reader." Sam is a "late reader." (Albert Einstein was a "late reader." Theodore Kaczinski was an "early reader." Not that I am at all defensive on the subject. *Pas du tout.*)

Sam and this woman's child were in the same class, and the next thing I knew, she had taken a special interest in Sam's reading.

She began the year by slipping me early first grade books that she thought maybe Sam could read. And Sam could certainly read some of the words in these books. But I resented her giving them to us with a patronizing smile, as if to say her child would not be needing them because he was reading the new Joan Didion.

I went to the God box. I got the piece of paper out with her name on it. I added an exclamation mark. I put it back.

One day not long after, she sidled up to me at school and

asked me if I had an extra copy of the book I wrote about being a mother. It is black-humored and quite slanted: George Bush was president when Sam was born, and perhaps I was a little angry. I had these tiny opinions. I wrote an anti–George Bush baby book.

So when she asked for a copy, I tried to stall; I tried to interest her in my anti-Reagan, anti-Bush writing book. But she insisted.

So a few days later, filled with a certain low-grade sense of impending doom, I gave her a copy, signed, "With all good wishes."

For the next few days, she smiled obliquely whenever I saw her at school, and I grew increasingly anxious. Then one day she came up to me in the market. "I read your book," she said, and then she winked. "Maybe," she whispered, because my son was only a few feet away, "maybe it's a good thing he *doesn't* read."

I wish I could report that I had the perfect comeback, something so polite and brilliantly cutting that Dorothy Parker, overhearing it in heaven, had raised her fist in victory. But I could only gape at her, stunned. She smiled very nicely, and walked away.

I called half a dozen people when I got home and told them about how she had trashed me. And then I trashed her. And it was good.

The next time I saw her, she smiled. I sneered, just a little. I felt disgust, but I also felt disgusting. I got out my note to God. I said, Look, hon. I think we need bigger guns.

Nothing happened. No burning bush, no cereal flakes dropping from heaven, forming letters of instruction in the

snow. It's just that God began to act like Sam-I-Am from
*Green Eggs and Ham.* Everywhere I turned were helpful
household hints on loving one's enemies, on turning the
other cheek, and on how doing that makes you look in a
whole new direction. There were admonitions about the
self-destructiveness of not forgiving people, and reminders
that this usually doesn't hurt other people so much as it
hurts you. In fact, not forgiving is like drinking rat poison
and then waiting for the rat to die. Fortune cookies, post-
cards, bumper stickers, everything but skywriting—yet I
kept feeling that I could not, would not forgive her in a
box, could not would not forgive her with a fox, not on a
train, not in the rain.

One Sunday when I was struggling with this, the Scripture reading came from the sixth chapter of Luke: "Forgive,
and ye shall be forgiven." Now, try as I might, I cannot find
a loophole in that. It does not say, "Forgive everyone, unless
they've said something rude about your child." And it
doesn't even say, "Just *try.*" It says, If you want to be forgiven, if you want to experience that kind of love, you have
to forgive everyone in your life—everyone, even the very
worst boyfriend you ever had—even, for God's sake, yourself.

Then a few days later I was picking Sam up at the house
of another friend and noticed a yellowed clipping taped
to the refrigerator with "FORGIVENESS" written at the
top—as though God had decided to abandon all efforts at
subtlety and just plain noodge. The clipping said forgiveness meant that God is *for giving,* and that we are here *for
giving* too, and that to withhold love or blessings is to be

completely delusional. No one knew who had written it. I copied it down and taped it to *my* refrigerator. Then an old friend from Texas left a message on my answering machine that said, "Don't forget, God loves us exactly the way we are, and God loves us too much to let us stay like this."

Only, I think she must have misquoted it, because she said, "God loves you too much to let you stay like this."

I looked nervously over both shoulders.

A couple of days later my enemy's boy came to play at our house, and then she came to pick him up just before dinner. And for the first time, while he gathered his things, she sat down on the couch, as if she had done this before, as if it were the most natural thing. I felt around inside my heart, and it was not so cold or hard. In fact, I even almost offered her a cup of tea because she seemed sad or maybe tired. I felt a stab of kindness inside, until her son came bounding out of Sam's room, shouting that he'd gotten 100 percent on his arithmetic test, and Sam had gotten *two* wrong.

"Traitor!" Sam shouted from his room, and slammed the door.

By bedtime, Sam said he forgave him but didn't want to be friends anymore. I said he didn't have to be friends, but he did have to be kind. At breakfast, Sam said he still forgave him, but when we got to school he said that it had been easier to forgive him when we were farther away.

Still, several days later, when the mother called and invited Sam to come play that afternoon, Sam desperately wanted to go. She picked him up after school. When I went over to get him, she offered *me* a cup of tea. I said no, I couldn't stay. I was in my fattest pants, she wore her bicycle shorts. The smell of something baking, sweet and yeasty, filled the house. But Sam couldn't find his knapsack, so I got up to look around. The surfaces of her house were covered with fine and expensive things. "Please let me make you a cup of tea," she said again, and I started to say no, but this thing inside me used my voice to say, "Well . . . OK." It was awkward. In the living room, I silently dared her to bring up school, math tests, or field trips; I dared her to bring up exercise, or politics. As it was, we had very little to talk about—I was having to work so hard making sure she didn't bring up much of anything, because she was so goddamn competitive—and I sat there politely sipping my lemongrass tea. Everywhere you looked was more facade, more expensive stuff—show-offy I-have-more-money-than-you stuff, plus-you're-out-of-shape stuff. Then our boys appeared, and I got up to go. Sam's shoes were on the mat by the front door, next to his friend's, and I went over to help him put them on. And as I loosened the laces on one shoe, without realizing what I was doing, I sneaked a look into the other boy's sneaker—to see what size shoe he wore. To see how my kid lined up in shoe size.

And I finally got it.

The veil dropped. I got that I am as mad as a hatter. I saw that *I* was the one worried that my child wasn't doing well enough in school. That *I* was the one who thought I was out of shape. And that I was trying to get her to carry all this for me because it hurt too much to carry it myself.

I wanted to kiss her on both cheeks, apologize for all the self-contempt I'd been spewing out into the world, all the bad juju I'd been putting on her by thinking she was the one doing harm. I felt like J. Edgar Hoover, peeking into the shoes of his nephew's seven-year-old friend to see how the Hoover feet measured up, idly wondering how the kid's parents would like to have a bug on their phone. This was *me*. *She* was the one pouring me more tea, she was the one who'd been taking care of my son. She was the one who seemed to have already forgiven me for writing a book in which I trashed her political beliefs; like God and certain parents do, forgiven me almost before I'd even done anything that I needed to be forgiven for. It's like the faucets are already flowing before you even hold out your cup to be filled. Before, giveness.

I felt so happy there in her living room that I got drunk on her tea. I read once in some magazine that in Czechoslovakia, they say an echo in the woods always returns your own call, and so I started speaking sweetly to everyone—to the mother, to the boys. And my sweet voice started getting all over me, like sunlight, like the smell of the Danish baking in the oven, two of which she put on a paper plate and covered with tin foil for me and Sam to take home. Now, obviously, the woman has a little baking disorder. And I am glad.

# GRACE

There's something so graceful about a huge unwieldy person who has found a way to glide. I remember Marlon Brando ice skating a few years ago in *The Freshman*, massive and shy and full of grace out there on the rink, or Jackie Gleason shooting such great stick at the pool table in *The Hustler*, strolling around the table to take each new shot in total presence, total command. And there's something so graceful about a skinny little kid with poor coordination who's running in a gangly, goony way, arms akimbo, knees knocking—this hopeless little kid who will always be picked last in school-yard games but who's just so happy to be running so fast, running the exact way she's running.

I know more about grace than I did two weeks ago. For instance, that Auden was right when he wrote, "I know nothing, except what everyone knows—if there when Grace dances, I should dance." I know, because she was, and I did: two weeks ago I was onstage with Grace Paley. (And don't ask how someone like me got to share the stage with someone like her. Maybe it is simply that sometimes out of the blue the water boy gets to toss the ball around with the quarterback.) And I danced. But the thing is that since I have admired her my whole life, I desperately wanted to dance beautifully, and I didn't. I was a little like Peter Boyle in *Young Frankenstein,* putting on the Ritz. But I did dance, because when all else fails, you follow instructions.

I understand that Auden meant grace in the theological sense, meant it as the force that infuses our lives and keeps letting us off the hook. It is unearned love—the love that goes before, that greets us on the way. It's the help you receive when you have no bright ideas left, when you are empty and desperate and have discovered that your best thinking and most charming charm have failed you. Grace is the light or electricity or juice or breeze that takes you from that isolated place and puts you with others who are as startled and embarrassed and eventually grateful as you are to be there.

But had he meant Grace in the literary sense, he would have been referring to Grace Paley. In 1970, when I was sixteen, the women's movement had just burst into the general public awareness. I am someone who can say with all sincerity that I owe my life to the movement, but as it first emerged from New York, much of its gospel was defined by grown-up daughters who did not want to risk having anything in common with what had been their mothers' entrapment. As a result, some of the language of the early movement contained an ugly rejection of mothers, of motherhood, of softness, of wanting to be in deep relationships with men. But at the same time, coming out of New York from the tenements and the Village and the antiwar movement was a short-story writer whose work taught me that you could be all the traditional feminine things—a mother, a lover, a listener, a nurturer—and you could also be critically astute and radical and have a minority opinion that was profoundly moral. You could escape the fate of your mother, become who you were born to be, and succeed in the world without having to participate in traditionally male terms—without hardness, coldness, one-upmanship, without having to compete and come out the winner.

She was beautiful, zaftig, and powerful; she was a mother; she was in love; she was a combative pacifist. That was Grace Paley.

I used to almost pant like a thirsty dog when I'd have a new story of hers to read. I drank up her generosity, the radical wisdom in her stories, the wonderful sense of perspective, grounded in self-forgiveness. She pointed out her own flaws and foibles, but it was clear that she was not bogged down in them, not caught up in the small stuff. Foibles are not worth hating—that was the point; what was worth hating were poverty, injustice, war, the killing of our sons and brothers.

She's still beautiful in her midseventies, with that dandelion hair and her no-nonsense voice. She reminds me of a durable desert shrub that the wind just can't blow over—low to the ground yet with leaves whose lacy intricacies surprise you.

And I love that she eats with such pleasure. She and I had a snack the first afternoon; her husband puttered around their hotel room while she and I ate. He picked at a salad and bread with no butter; she ordered and ate a plate of sliced fruits, pretty as stained glass, but she also sneaked a lot of shoestring potatoes off my plate, hoping her distracted husband wouldn't notice, and she clearly relished them.

We were scheduled to do two nights together in a row, in cities several hundred miles apart. The producers of the events, working together, wanted us each to read from our work, then give prepared talks from the podium. But this seemed so controlled, not allowing for improvisation or flights of fancy. An idea lodged in my head: why not let us be together in front of the audience, a couple of funny, feisty women hanging out together, jamming? I was sure that this was the way to go.

I had to convince the first producer to give us a shot at this. I've been giving variations on the same talk for a long time now, and it was beginning to make me feel like Peggy Fleming skating to a medley of songs from *Fiddler on the Roof.* Perhaps this is what Fleming's audience would want to see—left to our own devices, we often want what is smooth and familiar and instantly warm. Mostly we do not want to pay to watch someone sit with the nervous abyss onstage. I do not think most people want to see Peggy Fleming skate to *Carmina Burana* or even Ladysmith Black Mambazo.

I saw Peter, Paul, and Mary recently in concert. I wanted to hear them sing "The Great Mandala." I became frustrated and somewhat bitter when Paul Stookey began to sing an interminable new song about the Internet.

So. I hoped that the fire of truth would catch between Grace and me. The producer gave us a chance to make this happen. It didn't.

Grace and I read from our own works for a while, and then we sat down to have a nice intimate conversation with two thousand people watching. And it was a weird, glumfy dance—a private dance done publicly. We totally bombed. No wait, this is not actually the truth: I bombed. Grace was fine. Everyone agreed later that Grace was fine. Apparently I went on too long every time I opened my mouth. Also, I dominated the conversation, and, according to one audience member's written comments, was "shrill and narcissistic." But I couldn't hear the music, I couldn't remember how to play my own song. I felt frantic and frozen at the same time, so instead of something bold and improvisational in fabulous dance attire, the audience saw me do the St. Vitus' two-step in tap-shoes and a straitjacket.

Grace thought it had been just fine. "It was what it was," she shrugged. But I knew it hadn't gone well—even her husband said it had been a disaster. And my fear of failure has been lifelong and deep. If you are what you do—and I think my parents may have accidentally given me this idea—and you do poorly, what then? It's over; you're wiped out. All those prophecies you heard in the dark have come true, and people can see the real you, see what a schmendrick you are, what a fraud.

Alone in my hotel room later that night, I felt stricken and lurky and dark, a wallflower at the vampire's ball. I cried a little, then closed my eyes, bowed my head, and whispered: "Help."

Out of nowhere I remembered something one of my priest friends had said once, that grace is having a commitment to—or at least an acceptance of—being ineffective and foolish. That our bottled charm is the main roadblock to drinking that clear cool glass of love. I remembered what Grace's stories were all about: self-forgiveness, and taking care of one another. It wasn't far away from Jesus saying to feed his sheep. Now, I'm not positive he meant room service. But *maybe* he did. So I ate strawberries and melon and cookies, then put on the heat, and got in the tub.

It was amazing. I do not at all understand the mystery of grace—only that it meets us where we are but does not leave us where it found us. It can be received gladly or grudgingly, in big gulps or in tiny tastes, like a deer at the salt. I gobbled it, licked it, held it down between my little hooves.

The review in the newspaper the next day was not very good. But by then I'd figured out the gift of failure, which is that it breaks through all that held breath and isometric tension about needing to look good: it's the gift of feeling floppier. One of the things I've been most afraid of had finally happened, with a whole lot of people watching, and it had indeed been a nightmare. But sitting with all that vulnerability, I discovered I could ride it. I felt ungainly, the way Marlon Brando looked on those ice skates, but at least I was back on my feet. I had come through.

I don't know why life isn't constructed to be seamless and safe, why we make such glaring mistakes, things fall so short of our expectations, and our hearts get broken and our kids do scary things and our parents get old and don't always remember to put pants on before they go out for a stroll. I don't know why it's not more like it is in the movies, why things don't come out neatly and lessons can't be learned when you're in the mood for learning them, why love and grace often come in such motley packaging. But I was reminded of the lines of D. H. Lawrence that are taped to the wall of my office:

*What is the knocking?*
*What is the knocking at the door in the night?*
*It is somebody wants to do us harm.*

*No, no, it is the three strange angels.*
*Admit them, admit them.*

And by the time I arrived in the second city where Grace and I would perform, I understood that failure is surely one of these strange angels.

When both Grace and the second producer said they wanted to go back to plan A, reading prepared talks from the podium, I said, "OK." I just decided to cooperate.

And the evening went really well. Grace was honest and sweet and tough, and she made everyone in the audience feel like going out and fighting the great good fight. Also, she's absolutely the only woman I know who can wear socks with fancy shoes and a dress and still look great. It's the beauty of comfort. She shone. I was just me, which Grace said later was all anyone asked. I'd really wanted to be Cyd Charisse onstage, but as usual, if I'd gotten what I wanted, I would have shortchanged myself. What I wanted was acclaim, and what I got was Grace, lovely and plain in her faded dress and dark socks, smiling at me all night.

# Part Four

# KIDS, SOME SICK

I think I already understand about life:
pretty good, some problems.

SAM LAMOTT,
at age seven

# BARN RAISING

On an otherwise ordinary night at the end of September, some friends came over to watch the lunar eclipse, friends whose two-year-old daughter Olivia had been diagnosed nine months earlier with cystic fibrosis. Their seven-year-old daughter Ella is Sam's oldest friend: they met in day care and have been playing together for so long that I think of her as Sam's fiancée. Now out of the blue, the family has been plunged into an alternate world, a world where everyone's kid has a life-threatening illness. I know that sometimes these friends feel that they have been expelled from the ordinary world they lived in before and that they are now citizens of the Land of the Fucked. They must live with the fact that their younger daughter has this disease that fills its victims' lungs with thick sludge that harbors infections. Two-week hospital stays for nonstop IV antibiotics are common. Adulthood is rare.

Twice a day, every day, her parents must pound her between the shoulder blades for forty-five minutes to dislodge the mucus from her lungs. It amazes me that Sara, the mother—forty-ish, small-boned, highly accomplished—

can still even dress herself, let alone remain so tender and strong.

The night of the lunar eclipse, some of our neighbors were making little cameo appearances on our street, coming outside periodically to check on the moon's progress, as if it were a patient: "How's his condition now?" But Sara and I stayed outside and watched the whole time. It was so mysterious, the earth's shadow crossing over the moon, red and black and silvery, like a veil, and then receding, like the tide.

Ella calls her little sister Livia; she stayed overnight with us the day Olivia was born, and we cooked pancakes in the shape of the letter O to celebrate the baby's arrival. From the beginning, Olivia always got sicker than other babies; she caught colds that wouldn't leave, which led to coughs that sounded like those of an obese alcoholic smoker. But her doctor never found anything really wrong, and antibiotics always eventually cleared up the symptoms. Now she and I sit together in her room and eat chocolate, and I tell her that in a very long time when we both go to heaven, we should try to get chairs next to each other, close to the dessert table.

"Yes!" she agrees. She has round brown eyes and short yellow hair. What a dish! "More chocolate," she cries and throws me the ball she is holding—I tell you, this girl's got game. I taught her to love chocolate, which her parents still hold against me.

Whenever I'm out of town I worry that there will be bad news when I come home, that a friend will have come over to their house not knowing he or she was about to come down with a cold, and Olivia will end up back in the hospital on the two-week IV drip. She has a blue toy phone that she calls me on frequently. Sometimes when I am out of town, I imagine her calling me and chatting away on her phone. I was gone for a week of teaching at the end of summer this year, and I kept thinking of her. I almost called California to hear her voice. I was working too hard and staying up too late every night, and the people I was with were drinking a lot. I started to feel like a tired, wired little kid at a birthday party who has had way too much sugar, who is in all ways on overload, but still finds herself blindfolded and spun around for a game of pin-the-tail-on-the-donkey, and then pushed more or less in the direction of the wall with the donkey on it. But I was so turned around, so lost and overwhelmed and stressed that I couldn't even remember where the wall with the donkey was—or even in what direction it might be found. So I couldn't take one step forward without there being a chance that I was actually walking farther away from it. And it took me a while to remember that for me, the wall with the donkey on it is Jesus.

I didn't call Olivia, but I kept her in my prayers. I said to God, "Look, I'm sure you know what you're doing, but my patience is beginning to wear a *lit*tle thin. . . ."

A few days before the eclipse, I finally arrived home but only after Sam had gone to bed. I lay down next to him and watched him sleep. There was an ordinary full moon in the sky; I studied Sam by its light and felt entirely pointed in the right direction. But Olivia's mother had left a message on our machine, letting us know that Olivia had been sick again while I was gone. They had managed to keep Olivia out of the hospital, but it had been touch and go for days. Watching Sam sleep I kept wondering, how could you possibly find the wall with the donkey on it when your child is catastrophically sick? I don't know. I looked up at God, and thinking about Olivia, about how badly scarred her lungs are already, I said, "What on earth are you *thinking*?"

The eclipse moved in such peculiar time. Maybe it's that I'm so used to blips and sound bites, instant deadlines, e-mail. But the shadow of the earth moved across the moon in celestial time, somehow slowly and fleetingly at the same astronomical moment. It seemed like the moon was being consumed, and as if all the moons that ever had been were being consumed all at once. As if, in its last moments, you got to see the moon's whole life pass before your very eyes.

Watching Olivia watch the eclipse of the moon, I suddenly remembered New Year's Day, seven months ago, out at Stinson Beach with Sam and Olivia and her family. They have a huge German shepherd who is always with them; he hovers over Olivia looking very German. He was with us on the beach that day, chasing sticks Olivia's dad threw him. It was one of those perfect northern California days when dozens of children and dogs are running on the beach and pelicans are flying overhead, and the mountain and the green ridges rise up behind you, and it's so golden and balmy that you inevitably commit great acts of hubris. Olivia seemed fine—happy, blonde, tireless. Just a few days before, her parents had taken her to the doctor for lab work, because her colds were always so severe. But she didn't have a cold on New Year's Day.

Then two days later he called with the news that she had cystic fibrosis. Now, seeing her the night of the eclipse, her upward gaze of pure child wonder, I find it both hard to remember when she wasn't sick and harder to believe she is.

Olivia laughs at all my jokes. That night I kept pointing to our dog Sadie and saying, with concern, "Isn't that the ugliest cat you've ever seen?," and she would just lose her mind laughing.

At first, after the diagnosis, we were almost too stunned to cry. Olivia's family has a tribe of good friends around them, and everyone wanted to help, but at first people didn't know what to do; they were immobilized by shock and sadness.

By mid January, though, I had a vision of the disaster as a gigantic canvas on which had been painted an exquisitely beautiful picture. We all wanted to take up a corner or stand side by side and lift it together so that Olivia's parents didn't have to carry the whole thing themselves. But I saw that they did in fact have to carry almost the whole heartbreaking picture alone. Then the image of a canvas changed into one wall of a barn, and I saw that the people who loved them could build a marvelous barn of sorts around the family.

So we did. We raised a lot of money; catastrophes can be expensive. We showed up. Sometimes we cleaned, we listened, some of us took care of the children, we walked their dog, and we cried and then made them laugh; we gave them a lot of privacy, then we showed up and listened and let them cry and cry and cry, and then took them for hikes.

We took Ella and Olivia to the park. We took the mother to the movies. I took Adam, the father, out for dinner one night right after the diagnosis. He was a mess. The first time the waiter came over, he was wracked with sobs, and the second time the waiter came over, he was laughing hysterically. "He's a little erratic, isn't he?" I smiled to the waiter, and he nodded gravely.

We kept on cooking and walking the dog, taking the kids to the park, cleaning the kitchen, and letting Sara and Adam hate what was going on when they needed to. Sometimes we let them resist finding any meaning or solace in anything that had to do with their daughter's diagnosis, and this was one of the hardest things to do—to stop trying to make things come out better than they were. We let them spew when they needed to; we offered the gift of no comfort when there being no comfort was where they had landed. Then we shopped for groceries. One friend gave them weekly massages, everyone gave lots of money. And that is how we built our Amish barn. Now, eight months later, things are sometimes pretty terrible for them in a lot of ways, but at the same time, they got a miracle. It wasn't the kind that comes in on a Macy's Thanksgiving Day float. And it wasn't the one they wanted, where God would reach down from the sky and touch their girl with a magic wand and restore her to perfect health. Maybe that will still happen—who knows? I wouldn't put anything past God, because he or she is one crafty mother. Still, they did get a miracle, one of those dusty little red-wagon miracles, and they understand this.

———

Sara was in a wonderful mood on the night of the eclipse. The viral cloud of autumn was about to descend, though, and this meant the family was about to find itself more exposed to danger, to cold germs, flu bugs, and well-meaning friends. There would be constant vigilance, fewer visits, endless hand washing, extra requests for prayer. There are a number of churches in the Bay Area and in fact around the country whose congregations pray for Olivia every week. And maybe it is helping. Still, the specter of the cold season hung above Olivia's parents that night like the mysterious shape-shifting moon. Sam and Ella stood off by themselves like teenagers, Olivia hung out with her mother and me. We all stared up into the sky for a long time, like millions and millions of people everywhere were doing, so we got to feel united under the strange beams of light. You could tell you were in the presence of the extraordinary, peering up at the radiance beneath the veil of shadow, the intensity of that rim of light struggling through its own darkness. Olivia kept clapping her hands against the sides of her face in wonder, as if she were about to exclaim, "¡Caramba!" or "Oy!" When the moon was bright and gold again, she ran up the stairs after her sister and Sam, who were cold and had gone inside to play.

Sara very calmly watched her girls go, and I could see that these days, her daughters were the wall with the donkey on it. We stood outside for a while longer, talking about this last flare-up, how frightened she'd felt, how tired. And I didn't know what to say at first, watching Olivia go chasing after the big kids, coughing. Except that we, their friends, all know the rains and the wind will come, and they will be cold—oh, God, will they be cold. But then we will come too, I said; we will have been building this barn all along, and so there will always be shelter.

# TUMMLER'S DOG

My friend Neshama's regal little granddaughter Akela is four years old. Her face is big and has a rising-moon quality, since it is round and fair, as they say in fairy tales. She has huge brown eyes that take a great deal in. She is a wonderful mix of toughness and fragility on sturdy little legs, with a quality of attention and seriousness that can trip her up. Sometimes she's very thoughtful, very composed and canny. She has shoulder-length golden locks that are really brown, but she tosses them as if they were golden, and she says that they are, so we do, too.

From the very beginning, while still in her parents' arms, whenever she would see an animal, almost any animal—see fur and movement—she would clutch whoever held her and try to climb that person like a tree. Dogs were the worst. Maybe it was the cavernous red wetness of the mouth, those big sharp teeth, or maybe it was their unpredictability, their sheer animalness. Maybe it was that dogs are so in-your-face; when you're that young, your face is so small, and many dogs' faces are so big—just about big enough for your head to fit in.

Whenever Akela saw a dog coming, she began to hold her breath, and her eyes went blank with terror. Then the agitation began, and the panic—the loud panic. Akela's parents couldn't go anywhere without anxiety—not window-shopping in Oakland, where they live, not to buy groceries, not to parties—without it feeling like a stroll through the Mekong Delta.

Everyone always insisted that they had just the right dog to help Akela break through. Or they insisted that Akela's parents should get a puppy—and they had just the right puppy. But by this time, her parents had also had twins, a boy and a girl, so here was her mother already surrounded by her own kind of puppies. Akela was three at the time, and often there was no extra set of arms to pick her up. The world had already been a little out of balance before—just two parents and her against all those dogs—but the babies signaled that the world had truly gone mad. Her terrors grew worse.

Finally, at the end of their wits, her parents, who are quite middle class and not prone themselves to therapy, decided to take her to a psychologist who worked with phobic children. Akela called her the talking doctor, and she loved her. She was someone who paid undivided attention to her and who listened. She helped her with the world. The talking doctor understood all sorts of interesting things about Akela, like how she secretly felt about the new twins, over whom she doted. And she gave Akela's parents, who are not religious, a great faith that if they helped Akela to be brave one dog at a time, the whole universe would shift gently, and that tiny shift would be enough for the girl's terror to be transformed.

The talking doctor taught Akela to watch a dog approach and say to herself, "Here is a dog, and it will pass." Every time she saw a dog nearby, she still held her breath, but she did not disappear completely into the bunker because she was also talking softly to herself. She was whispering, "It will pass." She did not rise up newly healed, but flanked by her parents, she got a little rest here and there from all that had scared her. Incrementally—a quarter inch here, half an inch there—she began to make détente with the fearful red toothy place inside.

Then, on the Fourth of July, her grandmother, my friend Neshama, had a barbecue out at the farm compound in the town where she lives, which is a very eccentric sixties kind of place: *King of Hearts* meets *Easy Rider*. Neshama lives in the big farmhouse within a ring of smaller houses, cottages, and shacks. It all looks, as my son said once, a little broken.

The people who live at the farm and many of their friends came by in the afternoon for the barbecue, after the annual town parade. Neshama had told people to leave their dogs at home or at least in the car, but the day was hot, and besides, some of the people who live at the farm have dogs, and the dogs found ways to sneak outside. So there were dogs. Akela looked out at them grimly from the window upstairs, where she was hiding.

A friend brought along the man she was dating—who was also a psychiatrist, whom everyone liked a lot—but he did not know the rules and brought with him his huge, white, well-behaved dog. Once he was told about Akela's fear, he sized up the situation and said to her parents, "I think you want to resolve this situation once and for all! This dog loves children, and children love this dog!"

The dog was white as a cloud and almost as big. It had a red mouth, lots of teeth, bright eyes.

Akela's parents and her grandmother told the psychiatrist they were doing it their own way, keeping Akela company one dog at a time so she could practice being brave at her own pace. After a while they said that everyone had to put their dogs away, because otherwise, Akela would have to spend the whole beautiful day indoors.

Akela finally came down to the yard hugging her mother tightly and whispering, "I'm scared." The babies and the other kids raced around happily. Akela sat tentatively in various people's arms and scanned the bushes out of which dogs might—but didn't—come tearing. Gradually she began to relax.

One of the people who lives at the barn went and got his rabbit, which was in a cage. The babies, who were now about a year old, were enchanted. The rabbit's owner lured it out with a cob of corn, this great shy lop-eared rabbit, and the twins cheered. Akela watched skeptically. Someone asked her if she wanted to try to touch it. She studied it for a while. After a very long minute, she reached out one finger, as if forced to stick it into an electric socket, and touched the rabbit. She touched the fur on its back, and nothing bad happened. She was pleased, in her quiet, Queen Victoria way.

Then the party went on, and everyone had lots of beer and stopped paying such careful attention, and her uncle Robert's dog got out. The dog's name is Rudi Kazootie, and he's a little rat dog, black and white, cute in a homely way—some kind of terrier, with an overshot jaw, buggy eyes, and no tail. A soon as Akela saw him, she said firmly, "I want to go home." But she was sitting in someone's lap, who just sat quietly. Her uncle Robert jabbed her lightly in the ribs and said jovially, "Look at that silly dog, Akela!" Rudi Kazootie is a real vaudevillian's dog, the dog of a tummler, who stirs everyone up and makes them feel like they're on vacation. Rudi began eating a sparerib that had fallen to the ground. His head disappeared, tucked down against his ribs as he ate, and because he had no tail, he looked like a black and white football.

Somehow this was not so frightening to Akela.

The twins couldn't get enough of Rudi, gaping at him, patting him. Then someone thought to ask Akela, "Do you want to pat him too?"

After a long moment, Akela slid off her relative's lap, reached out the one finger, her forefinger, like God touching Adam on the ceiling of the Sistine Chapel, and touched the dog on the back. Everyone stopped what he or she was doing and cheered. She was holding her breath. Then someone asked, "Do you want to do it again?" And she did; then she touched him eight more times.

Robert gave her an old photograph of Rudi for her to keep. "You can show it to your friends," he said, "and tell them you touched him ten times."

She furrowed her brow and put her hands on her hips. "I will put it in my jewelry box," she resolved. The box is filled with jewels of plastic and glass and a swimming medal, which she won at her lessons for getting into the water. People walked by beaming at her with admiration, as if she had just hit their team's winning home run. Then it was late, time to go inside, and the kids got a bath, and every-thing was very ordinary again. People wandered by the tub and said to Akela, "You touched a dog!" and each time she replied in her matter-of-fact way, "Yes, I did."

Everyone was rubber-legged with fatigue and effort but buoyant too, and none of the children fought or cried, and that, at the end of a very long day, with three tired children under the age of five, is a state of grace.

# HEARTHCAKE

S ome people think that God is in the details, but I have
come to believe that God is in the bathroom.

I started to think this exactly a year ago when a doctor
substituting for Sam's regular pediatrician ran some routine blood tests on him because she suspected he was har-
boring a parasitic memento of a trip to Mexico. He was in
fact treated for parasites, but two weeks later when they
tested his blood again, there was still something wrong. By
then he had had blood drawn half a dozen times and was
so panic-stricken each time that he had to be held down by
a monolithic lab worker named Ira. Ira would be summoned from the back room, and basically he'd sit on Sam
while the lab technician drew blood. It was awful. But it
was a Parisian holiday compared with the next phone call
from the doctor, when she said, "We've ruled out almost
everything obvious. I'm afraid I went ahead and sent his
blood work to the head of oncology in San Francisco. The
oncologist has studied our findings, and wants to see you
Monday." I felt the top of my head detach, lift up, and blow
away like a painter's paper cap.

"Oh," I whispered into the phone.

"We need to draw more blood today, too," she said. I felt terror like I'd never felt before, and rage, rage: I saw myself cutting through her neck with an electric carving knife. I wanted to shout that he didn't have any more blood, that she'd already drunk it all up because she was a *pig,* and that she was not to bother us again.

"Oh, God loves it when you talk like that," my sarcastic Jesuit friend Tom said. "God calls the escort service when he hears you talk like that."

I called all our best friends, and everyone immediately started listing all the things it could be, besides the bad thing. This was the battle cry—that it could be any number of innocuous things—but I have been through a lot of cancer with a lot of people, and I'm definitely nobody's fool.

So everyone, including Sam's real doctor—who was out of town but who spoke to me by phone—and my doctor friends, all said I needed to stay as calm as possible because it was going to turn out to be OK. Tom reminded me that sometimes you get to see just how little you're actually in charge of. I told him I was never going to call him again.

I started to cry, and I cried off and on all day. I picked Sam up from school and made some lame excuse for my tears, and I offered him any toy he wanted in exchange for him giving a little more blood. We went to the lab and they summoned Ira, who lumbered out and sat on Sam while blood was drawn. When they were done, I took Sam off to the bathroom with me because I had to pee and that was when I first discovered that God is in the ladies' room.

Maybe God is in the men's room too, but I have been in

so few of them since I got sober. At any rate, I sat on the toilet and closed my eyes. It was incredibly quiet. Then Sam began to fill up urine specimen cups with tap water and to do various pouring experiments with them—pouring water from cup to cup when the brims were touching, pouring from one cup to another from many inches away, covering the mouth of one cup with another and trying to transfer the water without spilling any—or, the second time, without spilling so much.

For our various friends whose children have gotten sick, the nightmare always began with blood that was *sanpakku*. These friends also insisted that Sam's funky blood could be so many other things even though in their cases, the bad blood hadn't turned out to be any of the other things, the better things. The bad blood had turned out to be cancer, cystic fibrosis, brain damage, a heart that wasn't growing and was never going to grow.

Mostly these friends were atheists, so you couldn't fob off some easy hope on them when the nightmare struck; they had no truck with grace lite. You couldn't distract and encourage them with nice Christian ideas about heaven or with what our Eastern friends believe, that death is—as Ram Dass put it—a little like selling the old Ford. As I've said before, I believe that when all is said and done, all you can do is to show up for someone in crisis, which seems so inadequate. But then when you do, it can radically change everything. Your there-ness, your stepping into a scared parent's line of vision, can be life giving, because often everyone else is in hiding—especially, in the beginning, the parents. So you come to keep them company when it feels like the whole world is falling apart, and your being there says that just for this moment, this one tiny piece of the world is OK, or is at least better.

So in the women's bathroom at the blood lab, watching Sam contentedly do his pouring experiments with urine specimen cups, I decided I would simply show up and be as sane as I could, as faithful and grown-up. This decision helped me to back out of the tunnel of fear. I looked in the mirror at my worried face, but instead of fixating on the crow's-feet, the brand-new Harry Dean Stanton crease in the hollow of my cheek, I prayed. I asked for faith in God's will, for faith in God's love and protection. I prayed for my sense of humor to survive. I prayed for guidance, and studying my scared-mother face in the mirror, I suddenly got my answer: Go forth, I heard, and shop.

So we went to our favorite cheesy toy store at the mall. I had, after all, promised Sam a toy. We went to the store, and he bought a plastic toy that changed from a race car to an armed replicant if you knew how to pull hidden limbs out from underneath the chassis, the tail from the trunk, and snap the menacing head out from beneath the hood of the car.

There in the toy store, watching him tear off the plastic packaging, my mind raced with images of him pale and quiet and weak, and before I knew it, I had grabbed him by the hand and headed back to the women's bathroom.

We went into a stall and I sat on the toilet and he began to play with his toy, which was in its replicant stage. I closed my eyes and prayed beggy prayers. I suggested all sorts of really awful people he or she should go after instead of my boy, people of dubious political responsibility. Sam was making quiet replicant noises, windy and metallic like a breeze passing through rusty machine parts. He seemed entirely happy, whereas I felt like I was facing execution. An ache of homesickness came over me, for our old life before Sam's blood got funky, for the sweet functional surface of that life, for all the stuff and routine that hold me together, or at least that I believe hold me together. That's the place I like to think of as reality. Maybe it's full of lusts and hormones and yearnings for more, more, more, and maybe it is all about clutching and holding and tightness, but I just love it to pieces and it was where I wanted to be.

Instead everything felt so ominous, dark and frightening, as if we were hiding from someone in a cave. I suddenly remembered the cave where the prophet Elijah hung out while waiting to be either killed by Ahab or saved by God. An angel had come to him earlier as he sat in the desert under a broom tree, and the angel had given him a message. First the angel told him he should eat. This is one of my favorite moments in the Bible, God as Jewish mother: Elijah, eat something! The angel said he should eat, and then rest, and then retire to the cave and wait for further instructions. The angel promised that the Lord would be passing by there soon.

So this is what Elijah did. He ate hearthcakes and drank a jug of water and then went to wait in the cave for the word of the Lord. First he heard a howling gale, but he didn't go to the mouth of the cave because he knew that such loudness wasn't God, "and after the wind an earthquake, but the Lord was not in the earthquake; and after the earthquake a fire, but the Lord was not in the fire; and after the fire a still small voice. And when Elijah heard it, he wrapped his face in his mantle and went out and stood at the entrance of the cave. And behold, there came a voice to him." The voice told him God's will for him, what he must do to save himself and God's people, and this of course is exactly what Elijah proceeded to do.

Sam wanted to leave, but I felt safe in the cave with God and Sam.

Still, after a while I got up and took Sam's hand and we went and got some smoothies. You really do have to eat, anything at all you can bear. So we had smoothies, with bananas, which I believe to be the only known cure for existential dread. Then we got in our car to go home. I liked being alone with him. He was talking about wonderfully odd things. "If dogs had the heads of cats but still the bodies of dogs, would cats be afraid of them?" he asked. He seemed happy. He has so little armor, few bulwarks or patterns set up to protect him; sometimes I feel like I am made up of nothing but. I remembered then that the people I know with sick children have had most of these bulwarks stripped away, and when this happens, they were left with a lot of spirit, when they were lucky, or suicidal depression. Often both: I've been watching our friends pass through the latter and survive with spirit and mostly enormous dignity. I shook my head in wonder. These friends had been pushed down into the depths so entirely that it left them wide open and hopeless. Then their best friends would come by, and that would help them hook into something besides their own terror. Their friends' love turned out to be the sound of God at the mouth of the cave, a breeze to sustain and help guide them.

I spent the next two days taking care of us. We ate a lot of muffins in lieu of hearthcakes, and drank a lot of water. I went into the bathroom a lot to pray for patience. People came by, and sometimes they sat with me on the floor of my bathroom. It was like the old days when we were all on LSD and sat close and breathed together. It would be great if we could go in and out of this place without needing drugs or Ahab on our trail—go into the mystic or the eternal present or whatever we might call it out here in California. But mostly it seems like we can't do it when we have our act together, because we can't do it when we're acting.

I also remembered that sometimes when you need to feel the all-embracing nature of God, paradoxically you need to hang out in ordinariness, in daily ritual and comfort. What is that old song? "Same old, same old pair of slippers, same old, same old bowl of rice, same old, same old glimpse of paradise." I washed the windows so we could see the trees more clearly, I gave the dog a flea bath, I lay on the floor and drew with Sam. It took such great muscular effort to appear unruffled, to hide my fear about his health, that I thought I might get a charley horse. I was faking it, not quite making it, but not going under either.

And soon my prayers were answered, first when patience miraculously descended like soft, chick-yellow parachute silk. Before, I had been fretting and pacing while waiting to hear from the doctor. But patience is when God—or *some-thing*—makes the now a little roomier. Looking at the one beam of sunlight streaming into the living room, casting warm light on our pets, two plants, one old friend and a small boy drawing on the floor, I finally realized I was more or less OK for the time being—and this was an amazing difference.

And then two days later the doctor called with the great good news that she'd canceled our appointment with the oncologist in San Francisco. Yes, Sam had to go back for more blood work—had to be sat upon one more time by Ira—but she no longer believed that he was in any serious trouble. He was eventually diagnosed with a really uninteresting allergy.

God: I wish you could have some permanence, a guarantee or two, the unconditional love we all long for. "It would be such *skin* off your nose?" I demand of God. I never get an answer. But in the meantime I have learned that most of the time, all you have is the moment, and the imperfect love of people.

I called my Jesuit friend and told him our good news. He groaned with relief. "Oh, honey," he said. Both of us were silent for a while. Then he said, "Baby? Sometimes deliverance is as cool as the air in a redwood grove."

# Part Five

# BODY AND SOUL

In the morning
After taking cold shower
-----what a mistake-----
I look at the mirror.

There, a funny guy,
Grey hair, white beard, wrinkled skin,
-----what a pity-----
Poor, dirty, old man!
He is not me, absolutely not.

Land and life
Fishing in the ocean
Sleeping in the desert with stars
Building a shelter in mountains
Farming the ancient way
Singing with coyotes
Singing against nuclear war—
I'll never be tired of life.
Now I'm seventeen years old,
Very charming young man.

I sit down quietly in lotus position,
Meditating, meditating for nothing.
Suddenly a voice comes to me:
      "To stay young,
      To save the world,
      Break the mirror."

NANAO SAKAKI

# GYPSIES

I have this beautiful feminist friend named Nora who once said, "I've been thinking about killing myself, but I want to lose five pounds first." I was remembering this recently when I started liking a new guy. He liked me back but was just getting out of a relationship with a young woman. Young young—she was ten or something, or maybe she just looked that young in the photo he showed me one day. She was tall, coltish, alive, thin, raven-haired. Right around the time I began to think about this guy in the biblical sense, I was at my most incredibly unyoung. I was tired, squinting, jet-lagged, stressed. Of course, I told myself, there is beauty in being older, being a mother, there is beauty in the wise steady gaze. But I kept thinking of this young woman and how beautiful she was and how undi-lapidated. Later that same day, I went to a mirror and looked for a long time, trying to see the timeless glory of crow's-feet, the resplendence of having survived. Instead I saw a woman in her early forties who grew up playing all day in the sun. Who knew? Then I saw a woman who had had just a few thousand too many social drinks, and then there was the woman who became a single mother. And the long and the short of it is that I looked like a fabulous woman who was on sale at the consignment store.

I am trying to accept that I am actually m-m-m-m-m-middle-aged. And even though I am a feminist and even though I am religious, I secretly believe, in some mean little rat part of my brain, that I *am* my skin, my hair, and worst of all, those triangles of fat that pooch at the top of my thighs. In other words, that I am my packaging. Even though both feminism and Christianity have taught me that I am my spirit, my heart, all that I have survived over the years and all that I have given, still a funny thing happened after I started liking this guy: I looked in the mirror, and sighed, and thought to myself, I will cut my eyes out.

Then this little-kid voice, this Tweety-bird voice, said, "We need to pray." I sighed again. Eventually I lowered my face into the palms of my hands. I know you have bigger fish to fry, I said to God, but I need a little help with this stupidity.

Ten minutes later some friends called and invited me to a movie about gypsies, called *Latcho Drom,* which means "Safe Passage." I had no interest in seeing it; what I really wanted to do was to go to an action movie, something with a little tasteful violence. I may have been more scared about liking this guy than I was aware of. But OK, gypsies, I said to my friends.

I sat there in the dark waiting for the movie to begin, staring at the blank screen. From time to time I tugged on the skin of my upper eyelid, which I can now pull out about two inches, like one of those old roll-up shades. I ate a four-ounce KitKat bar in an attempt to console myself, and my butt instantly began to feel like a beanbag chair. My underpants grew tight and deeply uncomfortable. I started to wonder if I'd accidentally put on a pair of Sam's.

And then the movie began.

Those faces: the gypsies are all born old. The men are dashingly homely, as if cars have ridden over their faces. The young girls are beautiful beyond words, and the oldest women dance. But the middle-aged mothers look just like me and my friends—tired, baggy, in some need of repair. Their faces are exhausted from all that it takes to raise children on the tightrope of gypsy life. When you're on the high wire, you have to use every ounce of grace and skill and awareness and loyalty you can muster just to get to the other side. But that's the gift, to have to use that kind of attention and focus, and it shows up around your eyes.

They seem always to be walking. As with all nomads, if you don't keep walking, you die—so you figure out how to keep walking. This also shows up on the mothers' faces, the exhaustion of exposure, of making sure that the old people keep moving and that the babies are carried safely. The mothers, women in the last gasps of carnality, are the sandwich women, like us—taking care of their own mothers, taking care of the young.

But oh, the old women dancing: the old women who shine with the incredible stirring of spirit that has kept them lit over the years, even though the winds howl all around them. It's so different from when old women dance at our parties, and people nudge each other with their elbows because it's sort of cute and horrifying at the same time, like having the dead or hidden insist on stepping out onto the dance floor, like watching Great-Grandma Adrienne attempt the Macarena. But the crowd of gypsies—squatters and outlaws, outside in winter, huddled together at train stations, cold and exposed—stands around while the music begins to play. Then the old women seem to cackle, Oh, what the hell, and they start dancing. They've stopped chasing anything down, and you feel the rush of life force that this frees up inside them. Their gnarled witchy fingers are on the carotid artery of the culture, the link between the living and the dead, and in their faces and their bodies and their movement, you see the beauty of having come through.

Watching this movie, you can tell that the younger gypsies think the old ones are absolutely beautiful, visibly beautiful, like movie stars. These old women sing in their scratchy crone voices of bottomless sadness, and still they dance. They stuff so much into themselves—food stolen and shared, passion, care—to keep the whole system burning like a potbellied stove. And they do, they burn.

It's so sexy and intimate and stark that you almost have to look away.

Watching the old gypsy women most carefully, of course, are the children, the girl children.

There's a girl in the movie, beautiful like Anne Frank, who looks about twelve, but from another century, like all the gypsies look, as if they were living right on the edge of everything that we protect ourselves from. She's at the back of a very plain tavern with her much younger brother, and the two of them are watching the men drink. In this scene, there seem to be only drink and music but no food—maybe because the room is neat, with a rough-hewn cleanness, and food is messy. Or maybe because they are too poor to buy the food here. So the men play and sing and drink, and at first the girl just watches. The tavern is a place where no one else wants to be, so all these people who've sneaked through the system can sit and drink and dance here. There are only men inside, though, and this girl and her younger brother, all part of the large gypsy nation, people who have been told for centuries, "You're messy, you're dirty, dangerous, and you're not part of our family." So of course the sense of extended family is fierce. The younger brother is very solemn, tentative, but the girl watches, knowing, dark and dirty, smiling, shy. There is such purity in her face as she watches the men —and then she begins to dance. She's practicing. A sense of mastery comes out of her, like a strong shiny shoot, because she's been watching carefully and she knows the shoot is going to flower. And she is going to dance, dance hungry, dance full, dance each cold astonishing moment, now when she is young and again when she is old.

But if the fortune of the girl is in the newness, in being the bud, and the fortune of the crone is in the freedom, the lack of attachment or clinging, where does that leave a youngish middle-aged American woman like me? Maybe it leaves me needing to consider how wealthy I am in the knowledge that the girl of my past is still in me while a marvelous dreadlocked crone is in the future—and that I hold both of these females inside.

Coming out of the movie that night, I realized that I

want what the crones have: time for all those long deep breaths, time to watch more closely, time to learn to enjoy what I've always been afraid of—the sag and the invisibility, the ease of understanding that life is not about doing. The crones understand this, and it gives them all kinds of time—time to get much less done, time for all these holy moments.

So I've been thinking about how, realistically, I am probably not going to lose five pounds before I see the guy I like again, or have the little canopy above my eyes snipped off. And how what I am going to do instead is to begin practicing cronehood as soon as possible: to watch, smile, dance.

# THE MOLE

It all began with a mole on my ribs. Now, moles for me may be a very different experience than moles are for you, because the malignant melanoma that killed my father began as a mole on his back. So when I see a mole on my tiny personal self, I get a little edgy. I see *other* people with moles and do not necessarily believe that they are dying—for instance, after many years of therapy, I can look at Robert de Niro's mole and not instantly imagine him in a coma, or Depends. But when I notice one of my own moles that suddenly looks a little—what's the phrase—life-threatening, I make an appointment to see my mole man, my main mole man at our HMO, a dermatologist named Stephen who has been walking me through my moles for years.

I show up and show him my moles, and he usually has one of two reactions: one is that he claps his hands to his ears and opens his mouth like the guy on the bridge in Edvard Munch's *The Scream*. The other involves a series of gestures: first his face falls in a sad Buster Keaton way, but he forces himself to make eye contact and whispers,

"I'm sorry." Then he chucks me lightly under the chin and loads me up with free samples of skin lotions and acne products.

I had a routine appointment with him recently, right after finishing the very last revisions on a book. I mention the latter because the results were a vague postpartum depression and too much time on my hands. K-Fucked radio was on all the time in my head—out of the left speaker came the endless stream of self-aggrandizement, and out of the right speaker the report that my book was an unmitigated disaster, that my career was over, my future behind me. I would have to go to work for the Shoe Source to make ends meet, and then the pets would all die because I wasn't around during the day to care for them, and Sam would go insane with grief and grow up to be someone who harvests anthrax in petri dishes in the kitchen. With all of this to solve and consider, I found myself hanging around inside much too much of the time, because I wanted to be by the phone if George Lucas or Nelson Mandela called.

They apparently forgot to, or had been given the wrong number. But while I sat inside brooding one morning, the dermatology nurse from my HMO called to remind me that I had my yearly mole appointment the following day.

The next afternoon I found myself sitting topless in my mole man's office, while he looked at my moles with his usual mix of boredom and contempt. But then, abruptly, he said, "Hmmmm."

"Hmmmm what?" I asked.

"Well," he said. "You know what? I think I'd like to

remove this one." He pointed to a small mole on my rib cage. "There's something a little . . . *off* about this one." Off? *Off?* I felt suspended and vacuumy, like when you've been underwater for too long, or that moment when the drugs have just kicked in and you haven't had time to adjust to the fact that the kitty can now speak English.

"Excuse me?" I said incredulously. "My *mole* is a little off?" I asked, as if he'd said my butt was too big.

Now this man is not stupid, and he knows that he is dealing with someone who is perhaps *ever* so slightly more anxious than the average hypochondriac. So he tried to look bored and said, "Well. It's a little dark, and a little irregular, and what with your father's history, I think I'd just feel better if we cut it out. And biopsied it."

"Biopsied it?" I asked in this tiny voice, like one of the American gymnasts—a 1-percent-body-fat voice.

"Let's just do it," he said. "Next week, OK? Make a thirty-minute surgery appointment with the nurse."

"But I'll be *gone* next week, for a whole month," I said. Oh, my God, what was going to become of Sam? I imagined telling him that Mommy had a bad mole; that we would be celebrating Christmas early this year.

"Well, make an appointment for when you get back," he said.

There were no available surgery appointments until six weeks hence. And I know me: I would feel a little more advanced bone loss each day, a little less small-motor control. That night at bedtime I looked down at my mole, and now instead of it looking like a small sow bug, it suddenly seemed to be alive and spreading, like a stain. I was too young to die—or at least, I was too upset to die. You don't want to die when you're this upset—you get a bad room in heaven with the other hysterics, the right-to-lifers, and the exercise compulsives. But thinking of heaven made me remember something: that I believe in God. And I smote my own forehead.

So I wrote God a note on a scrap of paper. It said, "I am a little anxious. Help me remember that you are with me even now. I am going to take my sticky fingers off the control panel until I hear from you." Then I folded up the note and put it in the drawer of the table next to my bed as if it were God's In box.

A grown-up sort of peace came over me. I could feel it in the ensuing days, existing side by side with a heightened sense of symptoms. I developed pain in my upper jaw, which made me wonder what I would look like with most of my jaw removed like poor old Sigmund Freud, and then a burning spot in my stomach, which filled my head with scenes in which I was heroically full of good humor after the colostomy. But in between symptoms I felt pockets of trust and surrender, as if I had gone into total free fall and then landed gently after a drop of just a foot and a half.

I coped. I endured. I was perhaps a little more like Nathan Lane in *The Birdcage* than I would have hoped, but all in all, the hours passed without breakdown or hysteria, which, if you ask me, is a lot.

Two days later I went to church early, wanting an extra oat bag of faith that Sunday. There was another woman there already, named Marge, who is in her late seventies. She has a granddaughter with a tumor on her heart—*on her heart*—who is getting chemo and is doing OK in many ways, because she is loved and has a lot of faith. So Marge asked how I was doing. I hemmed and hawed and said that I had a dark irregular mole that the doctor wanted to remove, and that I was sort of worried because my daddy died of melanoma in the brain. And she did not say, "Oh, for Chrisssakes—my granddaughter has a tumor on her *heart*. And you want me to feel sorry for *you* because you have a weird mole?" What she said instead was "Honey, that must be so scary for you, loving that little boy the way you do."

I said, "Oh, you got that right, baby."

She said, "You just give it all to God. You just give it all to the Boss. We used to say in the South, if you pray, don't worry, and if you worry, don't pray. So now, why don't you and me pray?" So we did. It was vaguely embarrassing—I mean, honest to Pete, praying in a church. But afterward I mostly felt that no matter how it all shook down, we were going to be OK, me and my boy.

I went home and called a friend. I said, "I have a weird mole and I have to wait *two months* for a surgery appointment."

She said, "That's too long! Especially for someone like you. Call them first thing Monday and ask if there are any cancellations."

And of course there was a cancellation. So my HMO's melanoma specialist saw me that day. He studied my mole with his magnifying glass, and he made rabbinical thinking sounds, and then he said he thought it was probably fine but that he was going to take it off just to be safe, because of my history. And right there in the office he gave me a shot of lidocaine, cut out the mole with a small tool you might dissect a frog with, and stitched me up.

I had my eyes closed the whole time and grimaced at the thought of the pain I would be feeling if I could feel anything. "Aren't I being brave?" I asked.

"Very brave," he said solemnly.

"Will I get some stickers for being brave when we're done?"

"*Lots* of stickers," he said.

Then he put a bandage over the stitches and sent me on my way. He said the biopsy would take about a week but that he was 98 percent sure that it was going to be benign.

"Are those good enough odds for you?" he asked, smiling.

"Clearly," I said, "you have never worked with me before."

It turned out to be nothing more than a weird little mole, irregular shaped and benign. I had stitches for a week and they hurt a little, probably more than they would have hurt a normal person, but what are you going to do? Sometimes I found myself clutching the tender spot on my rib cage where the mole had been, cupping my hand over the two stitches like I was trying to keep my intestines from spilling out of the wound. But then I'd say to myself, "I love you anyway, old thing." And roll my eyes nicely.

The afternoon the doctor called to tell me that my mole was benign, Sam asked me if I had been brave during the stitching. I said I was *very* brave. We were sitting outside looking at things. And it was as if the lighting director had turned the lights up full force, because all these small things were showing up more brightly—a yellow house finch, the tiny pink buds of the scraggly wild rose, a patch of ivy on our dirty-blonde hill.

# THIRST

I knew by the time I was twenty that I was an alcoholic, even though I was not quite sure what that meant: Dylan Thomas said an alcoholic was someone you don't like who drinks as much as you do. I thought I was a good alcoholic, mostly pleasant, maybe too affectionate after a few drinks, perhaps a little loud sometimes or weepy, but not a burden to anyone except myself. I liked being an alcoholic; I liked drinking and getting high or drunk with other people like me—I thought of us as being like everyone else, only more so. More alive. Deeper. More in touch with— with what? With spirit—our own—and with spirits: of the times, of humanity . . . and all sorts of other bullshit we tell ourselves when we have lost the ability to control our drinking.

One day in 1985, I woke up so hungover that I felt pinned to the bed by centrifugal force. I was in the sleeping loft of my little houseboat in Sausalito. The sun was pouring in and the birds were singing and I was literally glued to my pillow by drool. I decided to quit drinking. And I was doing quite well, remarkably well, in fact, until five o'clock that first night. Then the panic set in. Thankfully, I had a moment of clarity in which I understood that the problem was not that I drank so much but that I drank too quickly. The problem was with *pacing*. So I had a good idea. I would limit myself to two beers a night. Two beers! What a great idea.

I went to the market, which was one block away, and got two beers—two beers, sort of. What I bought were two sixteen-ounce Rainier Ales. Now Rainier Ale is fortified—it's the beer with the merest hint of raw alcohol added. It is to beer as Night Train is to wine. Winos love it, as do people from Bolinas, which is where I learned to appreciate it. It gets you very drunk very quickly, and it's cheap. What's not to love?

OK, maybe the taste. Not all people happen to love the taste of rye bread soaked in goat urine. I myself don't mind it.

I took the two Rainier Ales home, and I drank one. I got a little high, but it was only 5:30. And I realized I was going to have to make the second sixteen-ounce Rainier Ale last until bedtime. So after I put on my thinking cap, I realized that if I was going to pace myself successfully, I might need a little . . . supplement.

Luckily, I had a Nike box full of prescription pills. I have had a number of warm personal relationships with pharmacists over the years. Also, perhaps, like many female alcoholics, tiny boundary issues. So I was warm and personal with them and they would give me speed and Valium. Anyway, I took one blue Valium that night—so little, so helpless, smaller even than a tic tac—and washed it down with part of the second sixteen-ounce Rainier Ale. Twenty minutes later I began to feel better, a little calmer. More whole. More like God.

Then I drank the rest of the Rainier Ale and discovered that now it was only 6:30. So I smoked a little dope and took another Valium, listened to "Layla" five times, and then had a second moment of clarity: it was wonderful to want to pace yourself, but two beers a night? I mean, let's not overreact. So I went back to the market and got a third sixteen-ounce Rainier Ale and sipped it. I had to take one more tiny blue Valium, and then a Halcion, which is a sleeping pill that they have banned in most civilized countries because of unpleasant side effects. For instance, it makes you feel like killing people.

So I was able to fall asleep that night at a nice early hour, like 7:30, and I slept like a baby and woke up twelve hours later, completely refreshed. Wow! I thought. This is fantastic: no hangover, no being glued to the pillow by drool. I felt like a million dollars. Whenever people called that morning and asked how I was, I said I felt great, which was true, and that I was on the wagon, which I believed I was, in the reform sense of the phrase.

At five that night, I went back to the market and bought three sixteen-ounce Rainier Ales. I bounced back to my house, Mary Lou Retton–like, sipped the first ale, took the Valium, smoked a joint, drank the second ale, took another Valium, listened to "Into the Mystic" ten times, drank the third ale, took the Valium and the Halcion, and discovered two unhappy facts. One was that it was only seven o'clock. The second was that I was wide awake.

Ah, I thought, here's the problem: every so often perhaps, I may need *one* extra beer. But I am going to *sip* that darned beer. So I walked to the market, a little slowly perhaps, because I was concentrating very hard on not falling over. Because that would certainly indicate that there was a problem. But I made it to the market. I bought one more sixteen-ounce Rainier Ale, and tightrope-walked back to the houseboat, where I sipped the ale, took another Valium, listened to the Duane Allman riff in "Layla" a few more times, fell asleep, and woke up twelve hours later feeling totally great.

By the fifth day, though, after drinking the first of my sixteen-ounce Rainier Ales, I began to resent anyone's attempts to control me—even my own. And so, as an act of liberation, I bought a fifth of Bushmills Irish Whiskey and had drunk it all by dawn.

It only took me one more year to admit that I could no longer control my drinking. And finally on July 7, 1986, I quit, and let a bunch of sober alcoholics teach me how to get sober, and stay sober.

God, they were such a pain in the ass.

Let me put it this way: I didn't love sobriety at first. I thought maybe I could find a few loopholes in the basic premise of abstinence. Maybe, I thought, after a few months of sobriety, you could successfully smoke marijuana again, or maybe every anniversary you got to have one glass of a perfectly chilled California Chardonnay.

It turned out that there were not going to be any loopholes. The people who seemed to find loopholes were showing signs of failure; for instance, they were shooting themselves in the head. Over time, two of my best sober friends, thinking they'd found loopholes, shot themselves in the head and died. This got my attention.

I was, in early sobriety, too sensitive almost to live. I was like someone with psychic tinnitus; every sound or word was amplified to the point of causing me pain. The wrong whisper could pierce me like a dog whistle. Because I had not had time to develop any real self-esteem—it had been a while since I had acted in a consistently estimable way—I found offense everywhere. For instance, early on I heard a sober person say, "Religion is for people who are afraid of hell; spirituality is for people who have been there," and all I could hear was an attack on religion, on *my* religion. I couldn't hear that the person was saying that I had already gone to the most terrifying place, to the land of obsessive self-loathing, egomania, and decay, but that now like a battered explorer, I was bravely trying to find my way home.

I was angry for a long time. I didn't know why these annoying people wanted to help me or why they seemed to love me even though I was whiny and arrogant and defeated all at once, the classic egomaniac with an inferiority complex. I finally figured it out, although I could not have put it as well as Sam did last night. He was watching *King Kong,* the remake with Jessica Lange, and toward the end, he said, "She loves him because she can see that he's lonely."

And that is why they loved me and helped me become one of them when I grew up. Sometimes I feel that they're like the clumsy deadpan kids in *Peanuts,* with their sayings and slogans—like Pig Pen, blinky and dense, or Linus and

Schroeder. But I love to listen to them tell their stories of ruin; I'm a sucker for a good resurrection story. And I love to hear of their efforts not to see what was as plain as day. I have a doctor friend, for instance, who used to shoot up sodium pentothal in his garage and then make a run for the bedroom, where he could pass out for the night; he was convinced he had a problem with insomnia, not drugs. I have a friend who could admit he was an alcoholic but then one day had to have surgery to remove pebbles from his forehead; the tiny stones got embedded while he was smashing his face against the pavement at the end of a cocaine binge. Telling me about his operation, he said with enormous hostility, "*Now* everyone's going to think I have a drug problem."

I love these stories because they show where we began, and therefore how far we have come, from the blame and delusions of our drinking days to the gentle illusions by which we stay sober. Now we understand that the blanket really *does* protect Linus and that Schroeder really *does* play lovely music on a toy piano, because both of them keep at it. They believe.

# HUNGER

This is the story of how, at the age of thirty-three, I learned to feed myself.

To begin with, here's what I did until then: I ate, starved, binged, purged, grew fat, grew thin, grew fat, grew thin, binged, purged, dieted, was good, was bad, grew fat, grew thin, grew thinner.

I had been a lean and energetic girl, always hungry, always eating, always thin. But I weighed 100 pounds at thirteen, 130 at fourteen. For the next ten years, I dieted. It is a long, dull story. I had lots of secrets and worries about me and food and my body. It was very scary and obsessive, the way it must feel for someone who is secretly and entirely illiterate.

One week after my father was diagnosed with brain cancer, I discovered bulimia. I felt like I'd discovered the secret to life, because you could eat yourself into a state of emotional numbness but not gain weight. Then I learned how to do it more effectively by reading articles in women's magazines on how to stop doing it. I barfed, but preferred laxatives. It was heaven: I lost weight.

All right, OK: there were some problems. I was scared all the time, full of self-loathing, and my heart got funky. When you've lost too much water and electrolytes, your muscular heart cramps up; it races like a sewing machine. Sometimes it would skip beats, and other times there would be a terrible feeling of vacuum, as if there were an Alhambra water tank in my heart and a big bubble had just burbled to the surface.

I would try to be good, in the puritanical sense, which meant denying my appetites. Resisting temptation meant I was good—strong, counter-animal—and I'd manage to resist fattening foods for a while. But then the jungle drums would start beating again.

I looked fine on the outside: thin, cheerful, even successful. But on the inside, I was utterly obsessed. I went into a long and deep depression after seeing some photos of people on a commune, working with their hands and primitive tools and workhorses, raising healthy food. I could see that they were really tuned to nature, to the seasons, to a direct sense of bounty, where you plant something and it grows and you cut it down or pick it and eat it, savoring it and filling up on it. But I was a spy in the world of happy eating, always hungry, or stuffed, but never full.

Luckily I was still drinking at the time.

But then all of a sudden I wasn't. When I quit in 1986, I started getting healthier in almost every way and I had all these women helping me, and I told them almost every crime and secret I had, because I believed them when they said that we are as sick as our secrets. My life got much sweeter right away, and less dramatic; the pond inside me began to settle, and I could see through the water, which was the strangest sensation because for all those years I'd been taking various sticks—desperate men, financial drama, impossible deadlines—and stirring that pond water up. So now I was noticing beautiful little fish and dreamy underwater plants, and shells lying in the sand. I started getting along with myself pretty well for the first time in my life. But I couldn't or wouldn't tell anyone that for the last ten years I had been bingeing and purging, being on a diet, being good, getting thin, being bad, getting fat.

I remember hanging out with these people, letting their stories wash over me, when all of a sudden the thing inside would tap me on the shoulder and whisper, "OK, honey, let's go." And I'd cry out inwardly, No! No! "Sorry," it would say, "time to go shopping." And silently I'd cry out, Please don't make me go shopping! I'm not even hungry! "Shh, shh," it would whisper. "Let's go."

I felt that when I got sober, God had saved me from drowning, but now I was going to get kicked to death on the beach. It's so much hipper to be a drunk than a bulimic. Drunks are like bikers or wrestlers; bulimics are baton twirlers, gymnasts. The voice would say how sorry it was, but then glance down at its watch, tap its foot and sigh, and I'd sigh loudly too, and get up, and trudge behind it to the store.

It was actually more painful than that. It reminded me of the scene in Kazantzakis's *The Last Temptation of Christ,* when Jesus is walking along in the desert, really wanting to spend his life in a monastery praying, secluded and alone with God. Only of course God has different plans for him and, to get his attention, sends eagles down to wrap their talons around Jesus' heart, gripping him so that he falls to the sand in pain.

I did not feel eagle talons, but I felt gripped in the heart by a presence directing me to do exactly what it said. It said it was hungry and we had to go to the store.

So that voice and I would go buy the bad things—the chocolates, the Chee·tos, the Mexican food—and big boxes of Epsom salts and laxatives. I grew weaker and more desperate until finally, one day in 1987, I called a woman named Rita Groszmann, who was listed in the Yellow Pages as a specialist in eating disorders. I told her what was going on and that I had no money, and she said to come in anyway, because she was afraid I was going to die. So I went in the next day.

I sat in her office and explained how I'd gotten started and that I wasn't ready to stop but that I was getting ready to be ready to stop. She said that was fine. I said that in fact I was going to go home that very night and eat chocolates and Mexican food and then purge. She said fine. I said, "Don't try to stop me." She said, "OK." I said, "There's nothing you can do to stop me, it's just the way it is," and we did this for half an hour or so, until she finally said very gently that she was not going to try to take my bulimia away from me. That she in fact was never going to take anything away from me, because I would try to get it back. But she said that I had some choices.

They were ridiculous choices. She proposed some, and I thought, This is the angriest person I've ever met. I'll give you a couple of examples. If I was feeling lonely and overwhelmed and about to binge, she said I could call someone up and ask them if they wanted to meet me for a movie. "Yeah," I said, "right." Or here's another good one: If I was feeling very *other,* sad and scared and overwhelmed, I could invite someone over for a meal, and then see if he or she felt like going for a walk. It is only because I was raised to be Politeness Person that I did not laugh at her. It was like someone detoxing off heroin, who's itching to shoot up, being told to take up macramé.

She asked if I was willing to make one phone call after I ate and buy time. I could always purge if I needed to, but she wanted me to try calling one person and see what happened. Now I'm not stupid. I knew she was up to something.

But I was really scared by the power the bad voice had over me, and I felt beaten up and out of control, scared of how sick I had somehow become, how often my pulse raced and my heart skipped beats, scared that one time when the eagle talons descended, they would grip too hard and pop me open. So I agreed. I got home, ate a more or less regular meal, called a friend, made contact, and didn't purge. The next day, I ate a light breakfast and lunch, and then a huge dinner, rooting around the fridge and cupboards like a truffle pig. But then I called my younger brother. He came over. We went for a walk.

Several weeks later, during one of our sessions, Rita asked me what I'd had for breakfast. "Cereal," I said.

"And were you hungry when you ate?"

"What do you mean?" I asked.

"I mean, did you experience hunger, and then make breakfast?"

"I don't really understand what you're asking," I said.

"Let me put it this way," she said. "Why did you have breakfast?"

"Oh! I see," I said. "I had breakfast because it was breakfast time."

"But were you hungry?"

I stared at her a moment. "Is this a trick question?" I asked.

"No," she said. "I just want to know how you know it's time to eat."

"I know it's time to eat because it's mealtime," I said. "It's morning, so I eat breakfast, or it's midday, so I eat lunch. And so on."

To make a long story ever so slightly shorter, she finally asked me what it felt like when I was hungry, and I could not answer. I asked her to explain what it felt like when she was hungry, and she described a sensation in her stomach of emptiness, an awareness of appetite.

So for the next week, my assignment was to notice what it felt like when I was hungry. It was so strange. I was once again the world's oldest toddler. I walked around peering down as if to look inside my stomach, as if it was one of those old-fashioned front-loading washing machines with a window through which you could see the soapy water swirling over your clothes. And I paid attention until I was able to isolate this feeling in my stomach, a gritty kind of emptiness, like a rat was scratching at the door, wanting to be let in.

"Wonderful," Rita said, and then gave me my next assignment: first, to notice when I was hungry, and then— this blew my mind—to feed myself.

I practiced, and all of a sudden I was Helen Keller after she breaks the code for "water," walking around touching things, learning their names. Only in my case, I was discovering which foods I was hungry for, and what it was like to eat them. I felt a strange loneliness at first, but then came upon a great line in one of Geneen Roth's books on eating, which said that awareness was about learning to keep yourself company. So I'd feel the scratchy emptiness in my belly, and I'd mention to myself that I seemed hungry. And then I'd ask myself, in a deeply maternal way, what I felt like eating.

"Well, actually, I feel like some Chee·tos," I might say. So I'd go and buy a bag of Chee·tos, put some in a bowl, and eat them. God! It was amazing. Then I'd check in with myself: "Do you want some more?" I'd ask.

"No," I'd say. "But don't throw them out."

I had been throwing food out or wetting it in the sink since I was fourteen, ever since my first diet. Every time I broke down and ate forbidden foods, I would throw out or wet what I'd left uneaten, because each time I was about to start over and be good again.

"I'm hungry," I'd say to myself. "I'd like some frosting."

"OK."

"And some Chee·tos."

So I'd have some frosting and some Chee·tos for breakfast. I'd eat for a while. Then I'd check in with myself, kindly: "More?"

"Not now," I'd say. "But don't wet them. I might want some more later."

I ate frosting and Chee·tos for weeks. Also, cookies that

a local bakery made with M&M's instead of chocolate chips. I'd buy half a dozen and keep them on the kitchen counter. It was terrifying; it was like knowing there were snakes in my kitchen. I'd eat a little, stop when I was no longer hungry. "Want one more cookie?" I'd ask.

"No, thanks," I'd say. "But maybe later. Don't wet them."

I never wet another bag of cookies. One day I woke up and discovered that I also felt like having some oranges, then rice, then sautéed bell peppers. Maybe also some days the random pound of M&M's. But from then on I was always able at least to keep whatever I ate down—or rather, in my case, up. I went from feeling like a Diane Arbus character, viewed through the lens of her self-contempt, to someone filmed by a friendly cousin, someone who gently noted the concentration on my face as I washed a colander of tiny new potatoes.

Over the years, my body has not gotten firmer. Just the opposite in fact. But when I feel fattest and flabbiest and most repulsive, I try to remember that gravity speaks; also, that no one needs that plastic-body perfection from women of age and substance. Also, that I do not live in my thighs or in my droopy butt. I live in joy and motion and cover-ups. I live in the nourishment of food and the sun and the warmth of the people who love me.

It is, finally, so wonderful to have learned to eat, to taste and love what slips down my throat, padding me, filling me up, that I'm not uncomfortable calling it a small miracle. A friend who does not believe in God says, "Maybe not a miracle, but a little improvement," but to that I say, Listen! You must not have heard me right: I couldn't *feed* myself! So thanks for your input, but I know where I was, and I know where I am now, and you just can't get here from there. Something happened that I had despaired would ever happen. It was like being a woman who has despaired of ever getting to be a mother but who now cradles a baby. So it was either a miracle—Picasso said, "Everything is a miracle; it's a miracle that one does not dissolve in one's bath like a lump of sugar"—or maybe it was more of a gift, one that required some assembly. But whatever it was, learning to eat was about learning to live—and deciding to live; and it is one of the most radical things I've ever done.

# THE AUNTIES

Spiritual experiences do not happen frequently at tropical vacation spots for normal people who travel well, but there is no one fitting that description around here. I wish I could get to Kathmandu for my transformations, but I can't get any farther than Mexico. I am too much of an alarmist to stay airborne much longer than that; I can only cross one or two time zones before serious decompensation sets in. I would love to go to the Caribbean someday, or India. But they're too far. In the meantime, Mexico is my training tropics.

So I was in the Mexican state of Oaxaca when I got my most recent brown-bag spiritual victory: I broke through Butt Mind in the town of Huatulco. Or at any rate, I have only had a mild case of Butt Mind since. In earlier incarnations I've spent days and entire weeks comparing my butt to everyone else's butt. Sometimes my butt was better-than, although it is definitely the butt of a mother who keeps forgetting to work out. Mostly it was worse-than. On tropical beaches it has almost always been much-worse-than. I did not expect things to be any different this time, because gravity is having its say. Also as it turned out, there were lots of teenage girls around, only a few of whom, statistically, could be expected to have droopy butts and major dimpling issues—the feta-cheese look, as one friend puts it.

I started off in heavy Butt Mind on the plane. I was with Sam and our best friends. There were all these teenage girls on board in tiny shorts that Sam could have borrowed. Someone less secure about her own beauty might have said, "Too many teenage girls." They were mostly youthful and bouncy and physically stunning, if you happen to find tan lean youth attractive. But I had recently read a magazine article on Junkie Chic, society's current exhortation of drowsy, skaggy emaciation. And for some reason the article was *mostly* making me feel militantly on my own middle-aged-mother-butt side.

I was also thinking of a priest I have mentioned before, who said that sometimes he thinks that heaven is just a new pair of glasses. I was trying to remember to wear them. I was trying to spend less time thinking about what I see and more time thinking about why I see it that way—why I continue, off and on, to see these nice sturdy high-functioning thighs with such contempt. It's so troubling to relapse in this area, especially since somewhere along the line, I have actually come to believe that a person being herself is beautiful—that contentment and acceptance and freedom are beautiful. And most important, I have discovered *I* am clinically and objectively beautiful.

I really mean this in the literal sense. I believe that if you saw me, you would say, "Wow! What a beautiful woman."

I think.

I'm almost sure.

But of course, I was thinking all these lofty things before I got to the beach.

Until recently, I was afraid to say that I am beautiful out loud for fear that people would look at each other with amusement and think to themselves, Well, isn't that nice. And then they would look at me with cruel scrutiny and see a thinnish woman with tired wrinkly eyes, flabby thighs, scriggly-scraggly hair, as my son once described it, and scriggly-scraggly teeth. I was afraid they would see the spidery veins on my legs and note that my bottom appears to be making a break for freedom from the confines of my swimsuit; afraid that they would notice all the parts of me that really need to have the fat vacuumed out, or at least carpet-swept. But somehow I was not afraid to say it anymore. On that plane with all these beautiful young girls walking up the aisle as if it were a runway, if someone had exhibited so much as an angstrom of doubt about my beauty, I would have said that they could come kiss my big, beautiful, dimply, droopy butt.

However, as I said, this was before I got to the beach.

After unpacking in Huatulco, I put on my best black swimsuit. It was very expensive when I got it, very alluring. The only fly in the ointment was that it no longer fit. Actually, I'm not positive it ever did, but at least I used to be able to get it on without bruising. There in my room overlooking the turquoise sea, palm tree groves, and a sky of bright light blue, as I strained to pull the suit up past my thighs, I consoled myself by remembering that there is beauty in becoming so comfortable at being a mother, and a writer; there is grace in comfortableness. And of the several things of which I'm almost positive, one is that if I live to be an old woman, I won't be sitting on my porch berating myself for having leapt into a swimsuit to swim in warm ocean water at every opportunity even though my thighs were dimply. Also, most helpful of all, the wife of the couple we were traveling with—our best friends—has dimply thighs and a big butt too.

Maybe even bigger. Not that I'm comparing or anything.

Anyway. I got my suit on and waddled down to the beach.

I was not wearing a cover-up, not even a T-shirt. I had decided I was going to take my thighs and butt with me proudly wherever I went. I decided, in fact, on the way to the beach that I would treat them as if they were beloved elderly aunties, the kind who did embarrassing things at the beach, like roll their stockings into tubes around their ankles, but whom I was proud of because they were so great in every *real and important* way. So we walked along, the three of us, the aunties and I, to meet Sam and our friends in the sand. I imagined that I could feel the aunties beaming, as if they had been held captive in a dark closet too long, like Patty Hearst. Freed finally to stroll on a sandy Mexican beach: what a beautiful story.

It did not trouble me that parts of my body—the auntie parts—kept moving even after I had come to a full halt. Who cares? People just need to be soft and clean.

The first girls I saw were young, nine or ten, splashing

around on the rocks near the shore, pretending to be horses. One of them was catching crabs. Iguanas watched with unblinking eyes from boulders that lined the walkway, and the three girls were fearless, unself-conscious and so lovely. At nine or ten, girls still get to be fine. They've still got a couple of years before they totally forget what they do have and start obsessing about what they don't. These girls had legs like baby egrets, probably not much changed from when they were seven and eight. They were still of an age when they could play without wearing the glasses of puberty that would make them see all their flaws. Not yet measuring, not yet comparing, still able to get caught up in crabs, in iguanas and currents, lost in what is right in front of them.

I was inspired. I found Sam and our friends on the beach, and we swam all afternoon, and everything was wonderful. Then I decided to head back up to my room for a little nap before dinner. Sam stayed with our friends on the beach. The aunties and I marched along in a way both strident and shy, until we got to one of the bus stops where the vans pick up people and drive them up the steep hillside. First I was alone, and that was nice, because I got to practice acting as if it was OK for a person with middle-aged thighs to stand around wearing only a swimsuit like other people. I smiled, thought fondly of the aunties, imagining one as Margaret Rutherford in old age, one as Samantha's dreamy aunt Clara in *Bewitched*, who could never get her spells to work.

And then out of nowhere, like dogs from hell, four teenage girls walked toward me to wait for a van.

They weren't wearing cover-ups either, but they were lovely and firm as models—I'd say that was the main difference—*and* all in bikinis. Two of them were already perfectly tan. And suddenly my trance was broken. Suddenly it was the Emperor's New Clothes, and I stood there in all of my fatitude like the tubby little emperor with his feta-cheese gut. In my mind now I looked like someone under fluorescent lights and felt in comparison to these girls like Roy Cohn in his last days. I wanted a trapdoor to open at my feet. And then—this is the truth—they *looked* at me. They looked at me standing there in the bright sunlight wearing only an ill-fitting swimsuit that had been laundered more times than the funds in Oliver North's campaign chest.

But then they made a fatal mistake. They looked at each other with these amused looks—the kind I must have given flabby women in swimsuits thirty years ago. And it gave me time to have two thoughts. One was not even a thought exactly: I just looked directly back at the four of them and heard the phantom clock playing in the background of their lives, "Tick, tock . . . tick, tock."

The other was the realization that I knew their secret: that they didn't think *they* were OK. They were already in the hyper self-consciousness of the American teenage girl, and this meant that they were doomed. The smallest one probably thought she was too short, the other one too tall. The most beautiful one had no breasts, the buxom one had crisp thin hair.

My heart softened, and I could breathe again (although I would have killed for a sarong). I felt deep compassion for them; I wanted to tell them the good news—that at some point you give up on ever looking much better than you do. Somehow, you get a little older, a little fatter, and you end up going a little easier on yourself. Or a lot easier. And I no longer felt ugly, maybe just a little ridiculous. I held my head a bit higher; I touched the aunties gently, to let them know I was there, and that made me less afraid. Ugliness is creeping around in fear, I remembered. Yet here I was, almost naked, and—to use the medical term—flabbier than shit, but deeply loyal to myself.

I forced myself not to check out their butts.

Finally, mercifully, a van came along and took us up the hill. The girls got off before me and walked toward their rooms. God—they had the most incredibly small butts. It made me want to kill myself.

When I got to my room, I took a long, hot shower and then stood studying myself naked in the mirror. I looked like Divine. But then I thought about the poor aunties, how awful it must feel to have me judging them so harshly—the darling aunties! A gasp at this injustice escaped my lips, and my heart grew soft and maternal, and then I said out loud, "God! I am so sorry," and the aunties tucked their heads down shyly, not knowing now if they were safe. "Oh, mon Dieu," I told them, and then, "Oh, my dears." I put on my sexiest T-shirt, my cutest underpants, and I slathered rose-scented lotion on my legs, rubbing it in gently with the indignation of a mother who has rescued her daughter from school-yard bullies or the hands of the Philistines.

I put on a little light foundation, as if making up a friend, a tiny bit of blusher, and way too much mascara—

there are times when nothing else will do. Sam barged in, sunburned and hungry and demanding that we go to the dining room right that second, but the aunties and I ignored him.

Because now we were putting up our hair.

"Why do you have to do that when I'm *starving* to death?"

He wouldn't understand: he looks like a cross between God and Cindy Crawford. And I don't understand entirely either. But I knew to put on my favorite earrings. I wasn't thinking that I looked awful and wanted to look like someone else; that is the point at which you can come dangerously close to female impersonation. I just remembered that sometimes you start with the outside and you get it right. You tend to your spirit through the body. It's polishing the healthy young skin of that girl who was here just a moment ago, who still lives inside. It's saying that sometimes maybe one looks a little pale and wan and wants to shine a little light on oneself. Then, when you're in that honoring place, it's almost like makeup becomes a form of light, just as on those days when a little cloud cover makes you really notice the sun's rays that come slanting through. Maybe the key is simply a wry fondness for the thing you're slapping this stuff onto, instead of a desire to disguise; so it's not that you're wearing a coat of paint, but a mantilla.

# Part Six

# FAMBLY

The heart that
breaks open can
contain the
whole universe.

JOANNA MACY

# MOM

---

An old friend took a photograph of my mother and me on Stinson Beach this year on the Fourth of July. We are holding hands in the picture, as in fact we were doing all day, because my mom feels very unsteady walking on sand.

She's in her midseventies now—short and round, with big brown eyes and cropped gray hair that used to be black and stream down her back like lava.

In the photo I am looking over at her with enormous gentleness, because I sometimes feel this. Some part of me is Odysseus's dog. But I was only feeling this about half the time that day. The rest of the time I was annoyed. I was annoyed in general because she is not at all whom I would have picked at the Neiman-Marcus Mommy Salon. I would have chosen someone tall, elegant, and physical. I would have chosen someone with a ferocious belief in herself and God and me. I would have chosen someone who did not give a shit what other people thought of her or her children. I would have chosen someone who refused—

with incredulity—to be the sherpa for any man's hatred of his mother.

Specifically I think I was annoyed that day because she acts so much older than she is. She is only seventy-three, but she staggers along in the sand like a toddler. I was annoyed because she had asked me once again with anxious hope if I had met anyone nice. I was also annoyed because dark pink lipstick was smeared on her front teeth. I was annoyed when I went to pick her up because she had taped even more photographs of my father to the wall, although they had been divorced for years by the time he died, after a long and disappointing marriage. I was annoyed because we were waiting for my younger brother and my son to meet us at the beach for a Fourth of July party at a friend's house, and each time my brother's name was even mentioned, my mother acted like a Frank Sinatra fan. Also, she is so needy: she needs me to pull her to her feet when she's been sitting down, needs to grip my hand tightly when she walks as though we are on a tightrope instead of a beach, she needs me to retrieve her lipstick from inside our friend's house. Her smile already looks like a distant Tahitian sunset. Also, I secretly believed she could do better if she tried, that—perhaps this sounds paranoid—she acts this way to torture and control me. In my worst moments, I imagine her at home just before I pick her up, wearing a telephone headset and berating some commodities trader. Then when she hears me knock, she dashes to her bedroom, stashes the headset, pulls on her Ruth Buzzi cardigan, applies lipstick to her teeth, and totters to the front door to let me in.

On the beach I hold her hand and feel that my heart

could break with love for her. Ten minutes later I find myself growling at her when she's out of earshot, when she's sitting on the sand waiting for me to return with her lipstick. I have become a person of growl.

Sometimes, holding her soft warm hand, I want to take it and hurl it to the sand beneath the wheels of the oncoming lifeguard's jeep. But oh, God, the trust with which she keeps holding it out for me to take! Without someone to steady her, she cannot find her balance. And I guess when you take away the resentment and disappointment, it's that simple. It is what we do in families: we help, because we were helped.

Now when I look at the picture taken on the Fourth, my stomach aches with a miserable sort of poignancy because she is so friendly and eager to please. For just this moment I look like I am in love with her and she with me. For this one moment, we are. I am learning very slowly to savor the minutes between us that work, that cut through my life-long hunger for a more perfect mother.

I was nearly twenty when I finally understood that years before I was born, my mother had taken her invisible umbilical cord and tied it to my father's ankle. This is what many women were taught to do, because it gave them the illusion of power and connection, even though it turned out they weren't actually plugged *in* anymore to a real source of sustenance; they were just—let's face it—tied to some guy's ankle. Then I came along and fell in love with my father, too, and he fell in love with me and let me tie my cord to his other ankle. So my mother and I were no longer plugged in to each other but separated instead by my father's legs. Of course, he must have hated having to wear us, like those radar ankle cuffs people wear when they've been sentenced to their own homes.

Then other women tied on, too, and my dad was like a low-slung Maypole of women who were slowly going mad around him, competing for the tightest bondage. My father could be passively sadistic with women, playing them against each other. But I think my mom and I both believed for a long time that if you untied the cord binding you to the ankle of power, your cord would whip and writhe like a loose live electrical wire. And you might never get plugged in again.

By the time the women's movement came along, my mother had already put herself through law school. Several years later, she and my father finally split up. She moved to Hawaii, where she opened the first women's law firm in Honolulu when she was nearly fifty years old. She was so good-hearted that she forgot to charge many of her clients, and her finances were always shaky, but she was very happy. We got along much better from a distance. Ten years ago, my brothers and I asked her to move back home to California. We missed her, and felt she should grow old surrounded by family. Some days we loved having her back, but other days it was time-consuming and inconvenient; like real life.

Nine years ago, when I went to tell my mother I was pregnant and was going to be a single mother, I came prepared to storm out of the room at the first hint of judgment or skepticism. But my mom cried out in joy. She has loved Sam ever since that day, and he has always loved her, too. For the first few years of Sam's life, my mother and I finally found a consistent closeness; we were mothers together on this earth—plus, I'd given her a fantastic grandchild. She was in heaven. Then she had to go and get old.

Now she wants to tie her cord to *me*. But I'm somebody's mom now. And I still *want* a mommy—I do not want to be my mommy's mommy.

I look at this newest photograph of us, and I see how deeply she loves me and always did, how much she has forgiven me for picking my dad over her, and her forgiveness hurts me beyond my ability to put it into words.

Sometimes people who've read my work send me photos of their families, and I tape them to the wall in the hopes that they'll help me remember that we're all in the same soup, and that they'll make me more forgiving. Who was it who said that forgiveness is giving up all hope of having had a different past? The pictures do help sometimes, and I'm gentler with my mother, more understanding. They help by making me sad at how hard we all try and how far short we fall, and the sadness softens me for love. I go around trying to do better by her, trying to be God's tender hands and eyes. Then she calls and says something annoying, has forgotten something that was important to me, and I fantasize about jabbing her in the head with a fork, the way you test a baked potato for doneness.

I love her so much it makes my heart feel sandy and peculiar, the way your teeth do after you've eaten raw spinach. I sigh a lot around her. I grit my teeth. I regress. When I'm not with her, I go around feeling like the world is a gigantic baby with AIDS, and I try to bring some humanity to that in my lurching and imperfect way, like a candy striper with corns and PMS. And I do pretty well—until I have to spend time with Jesus in his distressing guise as my mother. Then the whole thing can start to come apart like a two-dollar watch.

In the photograph, both of us look our very best. My mother looks like all the good things she is: kind, highly intelligent, pretty, with gentle eyes and smooth fair skin. But you can also see in her gaze the need to please, the need of an elderly woman for people to see that she is a very good girl. She used to wear a mask of makeup, so she didn't always seem as vulnerable as she does now. The makeup seemed to hold her together somehow. Now she's like cells in the process of division, which haven't yet settled back into place.

I think this is why the lipstick on her teeth bothers me. It tells the whole world, I tried, I missed, I have no idea it's there.

We walk a little further in the sand. My mother sees things in the sand she wants—a sand dollar, sea glass, shells—and points to them like she's the Queen Mother; I swoop down in a plié to pick them up for her. I know she misses the beaches of Hawaii more than she lets on, the sun and her friends in Honolulu. She has pictures of them on her living room wall. She's sitting with them on the patio at the yacht club, playing bridge under beach umbrellas, and in their company she looks like she has finally landed back on her home planet.

There is nothing more touching to me than a family picture where everyone is trying to look his or her best, but you can see what a mess they all really are. Frozen in the amber of the photograph, you can see all the connections and disconnections, the stress and the yearning. And you can see the pride in their lineage—in that big bottom lip, say, that went from grandma to dad to baby. It's there on their faces for all to see, and you can see how they love it—that big lip. It is their immortality.

There are pictures of the people in my family where we look like the most awkward and desperate folk you ever saw, poster children for the human condition. But I like that, when who we are shows. Everything is usually so masked or perfumed or disguised in the world, and it's so touching when you get to see something real and human. I think that's why most of us stay close to our families, no matter how neurotic the members, how deeply annoying or dull—because when people have seen you at your worst, you don't have to put on the mask as much. And that gives us license to try on that radical hat of liberation, the hat of self-acceptance; we're allowed to escape from underneath one of the fatwas.

The friend who took the picture of my mom and me on the beach is fifty or so and utterly devoted to her big family. Once she was showing me some of her own family pictures. In one of them, she is eating soup at the kitchen table with her daughter, who lives at a shelter in San Francisco, who drinks and is almost feral now and furious with her mother, although she accepts the $1,000 a month her mother gives her for expenses. The mother and daughter have the same mouths but different eyes—the mother's small and brown, the daughter's so pale blue that you wonder if they were darker until all that booze washed the dyes away.

We study the picture together. "Tell me what you see when you look at this," I say.

"I see love like she's under my roof, drinking my soup. I see love like she's warm and we're talking like human beings. I see love like we are two survivors on a leaky boat, together, wrapped in dry blankets."

I used to carry a picture of myself in my purse, taken by my mother when I was three. I'm all dressed up in my mother's long, fancy gloves, and I seem very spaced out. My mother caught perfectly the soft, inward face of the three-year-old girl, marveling at her good fortune, in ecstasy over her lacy gloves. I liked to open my wallet and see the child I used to be, who was not used to facing the world; I liked to see that sensuous baby face bathed in wonder looking out at me.

In our family pictures all through the years of my parents' tense marriage, we look like we've seen sorrow, with faces that are sweet and sad and bleak and glazed. There are many pictures of my mother where she has made herself as beautiful as she can be. She has gathered all her pride around her, and her pride is her family. I used to look through our photo albums and wish that we were one of those families who got their family pictures taken on ski vacations, or on the beaches of Hawaii, or even in studios with painted clouds as the backdrop, as if the family had been lowered down in front of it and could be lifted up again en masse when the photograph was done.

There's one picture of us squinting on a porch as if the world were too bright and we'd all been dragged outside too early in the day. We're smiling in the shadows. My father must have taken the picture because he is not in it. My mother's mother, who was just about to move to a convalescent home, wears a terrifying corsage that looks like a dark baby opossum has died on her breast. My older brother John has a crew cut, a bow tie, a sports coat, and a beckoning con-man grin, Glengarry Glen Ross Jr. My new brother Steve is in my mother's arms. The small girl, who's me, wears a forced smile, and I'm peering desperately up at my mother, like I'm willing to grin for the camera but what I really want is for her to put the baby down so I can crawl into her lap.

We have all these pictures of us standing in front of our old cars. There's one of us posing by our sturdy old Dodge, which my father had just bought for several hundred dollars. Steve was still a baby and is once again asleep in my mother's arms. Everyone except my father looks so tired, and no one wants to be having this picture taken; you see the dents and the shame in the car and our faces. But my father really loved this car; he got a great deal on it, and his pride gives you the sense that the big slate-blue Dodge will endure, and that we will too. Life isn't easy and the sky may be dark but if you have this car, then you're ahead of the game. The car is like the hard shell of a snail.

Steve and Sam were late getting to the beach, and I felt abandoned by them, stuck with my mother alone while they were having God knows what kind of great fun. But as we learned later, Sam had gotten bit by a yellow jacket in Bolinas, across the channel from where Mom and I were waiting.

Steve had taken Sam out for the Bolinas parade; they were watching with an old family friend, when Sam, riding on my brother's shoulders, got stung on the arm. He started to panic, but then the family friend split open one of her unlit cigarettes, shook the tobacco into her palm, and made a paste of it using her spit. Then she applied it to the bite as a salve and told Sam it would draw out the toxins. I keep picturing the scene of Jesus making mud in his palm with dirt and his own holy spit, rubbing it onto the blind man's eyes until the blind man could suddenly see.

Then, making them even later, Sam and Steve walked into a pretty stressful family scene at the home of the friend who was going to drive them to Stinson, where Mom and I were waiting. People had reneged on commitments to bring food, and the niece, who had said she'd bring dessert, had brought potato salad instead, and two or three people weren't even speaking to each other. But Steve and Sam unintentionally distracted everyone with the monsters Steve began drawing to amuse one of the toddlers; pretty soon people insisted on adding their own touches, flames of fur and teeth like railroad spikes, blood dripping out of the eyes, nastier and nastier until after a while, everyone simply started getting along, finding the little kids some juice, handing things to one another, a dish towel, the salt. Without using the word, everyone started forgiving each other again. Just like that, from the no of all nothingness: you have a big tense mess and out of it comes some joy. It must be magic.

Finally, Steve and Sam arrived at Stinson. You would have thought they were the entire Supreme Court for the fuss my mother made. My brother is very gentle and easy-going, he always got along with both parents, but still, my mother's total joy at seeing him fills me with resentment. When I arrived to pick her up that morning, she'd glanced down at her watch as if I were terribly late; I was right on time. Plus she was wearing her worst sweater and she kept it on in the car, even though the day was warm.

"Nana!" Sam calls out when he sees my mother. We are sitting on the sand by then. "I got bit by a yellow jacket!" She gapes at him, makes sympathetic noises, admires the bite as if it is a bullet hole. "I didn't hardly cry," he tells her. ("He was hysterical," my brother whispers to me.)

She holds out her hands for my brother and me to pull her to her feet. She is still wearing the horrible cardigan, and the day is even hotter now. But I understand all of a sudden that my family is like this old sweater—it keeps unraveling, but then someone figures out how to sew it up one more time; it has lumps and then it unravels again, but you can still wear it; and it still keeps away the chill.

Besides, who made me the keeper of my mother's thermostat?

My mother turns to Sam. "Let's go for a walk," she says. He doesn't want to. He always wants to race down to the shore and just plunge in. But he's glad to be with her. The fact that she's wearing a sweater does not seem to annoy him. I watch carefully. I tell you, families are definitely the training ground for forgiveness. At some point you pardon the people in your family for being stuck together in all their weirdness, and when you can do that, you can learn to pardon anyone. Even yourself, eventually. It's like learning to drive on an old car with a tricky transmission: if you can master shifting gears on that, you can learn to drive anything. I keep watching. Sam takes his grandmother's hand. I feel like sobbing with grief that my mother is old, that she won't always be around, and with despair at what an erratic daughter I am. But it's not a big deal to Sam. He just wants to help her find her balance.

# DAD

---

I was in Houston not long ago, and maybe the city was just having a bad weekend because frankly, it did not seem to be working at all. Perhaps it will someday; perhaps it is going to be a hell of a city when they get it finished. As it was, it was like being there on the first day that the city was open to the public, with all of the bugs in the system revealed. But ironically, once again, in the middle of so many things being defective or inadequate, something old inside me got healed.

I was there with a man with whom I was in love at the time, although things were beginning to fall apart. We were dancing as fast as we could to stay together—because we were both deeply in love—but the effort left me in a state of isometric stress. I felt skittish and heavy at the same time, like a rhino. So at first it was fun and definitely distracting to find that the entire city was on the fritz. It was like being trapped inside a Buñuel movie; everywhere we went, everything went hilariously wrong. Our routes were staffed by stunningly incompetent people—by a cheerful young cabbie with no front teeth, no sense of direction, no map, and a broken radio; by hot-dog vendors so unhappy in their work that in previous lives they must have been calves, or Hindu. At one point we called a cab from a cafeteria to take us to our hotel, but not one employee knew the address to give to the taxi dispatcher. And we tried to buy some CDs at a record store where the clerk, with enormous hostility, refused to concede that she did not know how to work the cash register.

It was raining, and I began to feel even more subdued and anxious. I can do one or the other with a certain aplomb, but the mixed-grill effect is always disconcerting. And I suddenly felt like I was dodging something, something that had a pulse and was gaining. Somehow it was tied to my romance being in trouble, with having failed once again to get my father's dog suit to fit this man. He did not want to wear it; it did not fit him any better than it had any of the other men I have loved since my daddy died. This man was angry with me a lot of the time, although like my father he never raised his voice. I don't remember my dad raising his voice once in the twenty-five years I knew him. The man I was with grew annoyed with my fears and tears and my trying so hard not to be annoying. It was awful. It was awful for him too, and for both of us, I think it was home sweet home.

Now, there were at least three major areas in which this man and I were totally incompatible. But this was not the point: the point was that the thing inside me seemed to be hurtling itself against the walls of its terrarium, and I was throwing everything I had at it to get it to lie back down. To not make trouble, because I didn't want the man to leave, or freeze me out, which is, of course, the same thing. I was trying to be the perfect flight attendant, which had never worked before and which was not working now.

The dog suit was old and had fleas. There was no way it would be comfortable to wear.

I understood to a certain extent that these men of mine were innocent bystanders in my old family drama. But this didn't make the romantic problems hurt any less. The roar of the impending emptiness was almost dizzying. And I couldn't stop doing what I'd always done: I picked up the pace a little. We went to a lot of action movies, had another espresso, hopped back in bed, picked small fights just to get the adrenaline flowing again. I've found in these situations it's sometimes good to set a small diversionary fire, maybe tell your partner something especially heinous about your sexual past, or get honest suddenly about one verbal tic that affects you like tinfoil on a filling. It's all a way of avoiding the coming loneliness and the frightening silence inside.

But just when I was feeling my most wild and unbalanced in Houston, we ended up at the Rothko Chapel. A small ecumenical sanctuary designed by the great abstract painter Mark Rothko, it is a deeply sacred space. It is preternaturally quiet, like being inside the mind of someone whose eyes are closed while he or she is praying. There are huge Rothko canvases on the walls, purple and wine red so dark as to seem almost black, and what at first seems to be flat dark color soon appears to have images pushing through, like the shroud of Turin. The silence was pristine.

I felt like the thing inside was conspiring to get me to

*stop*—to make me stay in the extreme discomfort. I've heard it said that the Holy Spirit very rarely respects one's comfort zones. My boyfriend sat beside me. I could feel him growing antsy, and the shadow girl inside me wanted to leap up geisha-like and go off with him to more exciting venues. But this thing was pushing against me, and I almost couldn't move or breathe. I didn't break the silence.

It was as if something was going on that somehow had to do with why I was with this man to begin with. It was going to give me something I couldn't get any other way and that I didn't actually want. I didn't want it because it was going to hurt like hell, and I might not be able to stay with this man once I got it. And I adored this man. I understood that it was going to have to do once again with having tried to get a man to fill the hole that began in childhood and that my dad's death widened. I could smell the man I was with, his maleness, cigarette smoke, red wine he'd had for dinner the night before, all mixed with Irish Spring soap. I closed my eyes. I saw my dad sitting here beside me. He loved silence; he had begun to meditate in his midforties. He read me Wallace Stevens's great poem "Thirteen Ways of Looking at a Blackbird" a dozen times over the years; he sent me this one stanza on a postcard when I was in college:

> *I do not know which to prefer,*
> *The beauty of inflections*
> *Or the beauty of innuendoes,*
> *The blackbird whistling*
> *Or just after.*

The man I was with, however, loved music and talking and audible energy of any kind. Except when he was working, he often found silence unnerving. Silence is tough at first, like an infant is tough. I think it springs from the same place in the universe where space is made, and breath, and appreciation. I felt that the magic in the chapel lulled me into resting in a kind of hammock in that place where silence comes from. I let down my guard, and that turned out to be my mistake, because the thing was very close now and about to catch up with me there in all that stillness.

Right before it did, right before it pounced, I recalled the stillness of my father's office when I'd first step in every afternoon. I used to race home to see him after school, down in his study writing; it would be so quiet in there. He'd be thinking, scribbling away with a pencil. He'd have been typing all morning, and in the afternoon, he'd go over his work line by line, and when you opened the door, you'd hear his pencil on paper, a quiet scratchy sound. He'd almost always be happy to see me. He could make me feel great. It's so different having a living father who loves you, even someone complex and imperfect. After your father dies, defeat becomes pretty defeating. When he's still alive, there are setbacks and heartbreak, but you're still the apple of someone's eye.

My boyfriend finally got up. "Are you ready to go?" he whispered, not wanting to break the surface of that silence, and I shook my head. "I'll meet you in the museum," he said, and that was the wrong answer. The right answer was "I will sit here at your side forever, I will never leave you." I nearly screamed, "No! Don't go!" My chest was filling up with pain like water, and I called out in my head, "Come back, don't go!" as if he were leaving on a freighter for Greenland or crossing over from coma to death. Come back. Come back. I could hardly breathe as I watched him walk away.

And the thing inside was upon me finally, a silent and muscular jungle cat. I was almost gasping with dread, and then the thing started pushing out through me, like the images pushing through the Rothko panels. And right then, as brightly as electricity lights up the night sky, I understood that the man I was calling for could never ever come back. Because I understood that the man I was calling for was dead.

It was terrible. Just terrible. It was so stark that I felt as if the woman at the front desk had handed me a phone with one of my brothers on the other end telling me that out of the blue our father had just died. I almost began to keen with grief. How could you even *begin* to live with this desolation, with no longer having the love of your father?

I started to cry then, and I cried for a long time without making much noise. I cried and cried like a little kid.

Then the chapel door opened and I thought it was my lover having intuitively felt my huge need for comfort. But it was a much younger man, who smiled gently and sat down at the far end of the room on a meditation pillow. I wanted to cry out that my *father* had just died. But I was too stunned. And I worried that he would think I was nuts, because my dad had died in 1979.

Twenty years ago. For twenty years I have ached to go back home, when there was nobody there to whom I could return.

There in the chapel it felt like a drawstring was finally pulled, drawing together those twenty years of yearning into this one moment. I'd always known that one day it would happen, and I had even wanted it to, in an abstract way—you should see some of the men my girlfriends have stayed with for years to avoid this reckoning. Bad men, sadistic men, any port in a storm. But I was not ready for it to happen when I felt so profoundly alone; two thousand miles from home, with a strange man meditating on the floor twenty feet away from me; I could not have felt less ready to release my father's body bag to the mortician. But I did do that, in the chapel's silence.

I handed over my hope and belief that I did not have to have a dead father. Or that any of these men I'd taken hostage would fit into the space my dad had left behind. I handed over the conviction that I could jolly and massage them into being more consistent and kind so we could be together forever. I was devastated because I somehow knew this man and I were on borrowed time. But I have to say, I also felt a rivulet of hope inside me that somewhere down the road I might finally have a shot at love. Right now I didn't feel that I'd ever have that stamina again, but this was because I was grieving: my *father* had just died. The wind had been all but knocked out of me. Even so, I heard something Sam said once when I fell down hard on roller skates, so hard that tears had sprung to my eyes. He said, "You can't give up, Mama. You just gotta get right back up on your hind legs and try again."

The light in the Rothko Chapel was very beautiful; it bathed me. The face of the man who was meditating was soft and rosy, like he was giving off the chapel's light and it was wafting over to where I sat. The thing about light is that it really isn't yours; it's what you gather and shine back. And it gets more power from reflectiveness; if you sit still and take it in, it fills your cup, and then you can give it off yourself. So I sat still. The young man's legs were impossibly long, yet he continued to sit cross-legged, eyes closed, silent. My father had long legs, too. I tried very hard to keep up with him when I was a child. That's why I naturally walk so fast, and why I sometimes feel I can walk forever.

# SISTER

I was in St. Louis recently, and something for which I've waited a lifetime happened: people asked me how they could get their hair to look like mine. I have dreadlocks now. I finally have fabulous hair. Now, you may need a little background on this to help you see why this means such a great deal to me: you've got to realize I grew up with men and boys asking me if I'd stuck my finger in a light socket. Of course, it's one thing when you're a twelve-year-old girl with nappy hair and the older boys ask if you've stuck your finger in the light socket; this is certainly exhilarating enough and could give a girl enough confidence literally to *soar* through puberty. But it's another when you have to keep fending off the question well into your twenties and thirties. At a funeral not long ago, in my forties, an old friend of the woman who'd died actually asked me if I'd stuck my finger into a socket. At a funeral! And his wife had to stand beside him trying to look as if this were the most amusing thing you could possibly say at a funeral. I looked at her with compassion, and then at him rather blankly, and said as gently as I could, "What a rude, rude thing to say."

I was a towheaded child with bushy urchin hair. My father and some of my chosen mothers thought my hair was beautiful, but they were about the only ones who did. I got teased a lot. My mother took me to get it straightened for a while; I slept on rollers for years, brushed it into pigtails that I tied with pretty ribbons, set the bangs with enough gel to caulk a bathtub, and finally got it cut into an Afro in the late sixties. It looked better, but I loved having bangs, and they seemed to be forever a pipe dream.

Industrial-strength mousse came along in my twenties, and I could moussify my hair and bangs into submission with this space-age antifrizz shit that may turn out someday to have been carcinogenic. I used to worry about this, but then I'd think, I don't really care as long as they don't take it off the market.

When I first started going to St. Andrew, most of the thirty or so women at my church who are African-American processed their hair, and still do. A few wear short Afros, a few wear braided extensions; but mostly they get it straightened or flattened against their heads into marcel waves. When I got dreadlocks a few years ago, the other women were ambivalent at first. I think it made them a little afraid for me.

Dreadlocks make people wonder if you're trying to be rebellious. It's not as garbling and stapled as a tongue stud, say, or as snaky as tattoos. But dreadlocks make you look a little like Medusa, because they writhe and appear to have a life of their own, and that's scary. These women at my church love me more than life itself, and they want me to move safely through the world. They want me to pass. So they worried, and slipped the names of black beauty salons into our conversations.

When I first started coming to this church, I wore my hair like I'd worn it for years, shoulder length and ringletty—or at any rate, ringletty if there was an absence of wind, rain, or humidity. In the absence of weather, with a lot of mousse on hand, I could get it to fall just right so that it would not be too frizzy and upsetting—although "fall" is perhaps not the right word. "Appear to fall" is close. "Shellacked into the illusion of 'falling'" is even closer. Weather was the enemy. I could leave the house with bangs down to my eyebrows, moussed and frozen into place like the plastic sushi in the windows of Japanese restaurants, and after five minutes in rain or humidity, I'd look like Ronald McDonald.

Can you imagine the hopelessness of trying to live a spiritual life when you're secretly looking up at the skies not for illumination or direction but to gauge, miserably, the odds of rain? Can you imagine how discouraging it was for me to live in fear of weather, of drizzle or downpour? Because Christianity is *about* water: "Everyone that thirsteth, come ye to the waters." It's about baptism, for God's sake. It's about full immersion, about falling into something elemental and *wet*. Most of what we do in worldly life is geared toward our staying dry, looking good, not going under. But in baptism, in lakes and rain and tanks and fonts, you agree to do something that's a little sloppy because at the same time it's also holy, and absurd. It's about surrender, giving in to all those things we can't control; it's a willingness to let go of balance and decorum and get *drenched*.

There's something so tender about this to me, about being willing to have your makeup wash off, your eyes tear up, your nose start to run. It's tender partly because it harkens back to infancy, to your mother washing your face with love and lots of water, tending to you, making you clean all over again. And in the Christian experience of baptism, the hope is that when you go under and you come out, maybe a little disoriented, you haven't dragged the old day along behind you. The hope, the belief, is that a new day is upon you now. A day when you are emboldened to take God at God's word about cleanness and protection: "When thou passeth through the water, I will be with thee; and through the rivers, they shall not overflow thee."

Obviously, when you really want this companionship and confidence but you're worried about your bangs shrinking up like fern fronds, you've got a problem on your hands.

Furthermore, I don't think you're supposed to devote so much of your prayer life to the desperate hope that there not be any weather. Also, to the hope that no one trick you into getting into a convertible and then suddenly insist on putting the top down. Because I tell you, you take a person with fluffy wiry hair like mine and you put her in a convertible with the top down, the person gets out of the car looking like Buckwheat. Or Don King. It helps in one way to wear a hat, but when you take it off you have terrible hat hair—it looks like a cartoon mouse has been driving a little steamroller around your head. And you can't wear a scarf or you end up looking like your Aunt Bev. So you have to pick—Don King, or Bev.

So that's the background. Now I have dreadlocks, long

blondish dreadlocks, and some of the people of St. Louis were asking me how they could get their hair to dread. All right, not many of them, but two of them, two straight white normal-looking middle-aged people. Mostly, people see someone with dreadlocks, especially a white person with dreadlocks, and assume that the person's hair carries with it a position or a message—the message being, Maybe you don't have as many prejudices against me as you do against black people, but you should. Most people, if asked, might wonder if perhaps dreadlocks are somewhat unpatriotic—isn't it unpatriotic not to comb your hair? The tangles are so funky, and who knows, they may harbor bugs and disease. Perhaps to some people dreadlocks indicate confusion of thought and character: good children have shiny combed hair, while bad children, poor children, loser kids, have bushy hair.

But two people in St. Louis stopped me on the street and asked for instructions on how to get their hair to look like mine.

Eight years after I joined St. Andrew, I moved to a new neighborhood north of where we'd been living. The bad news was that there was more weather there. Hotter weather, more humid weather, fern-frond-bangs weather. The good news was that a large, beautiful radical African-American Buddhist professor named Marlene Jones Schoonover lived there too, and she had the most beautiful dreadlocks—lovely playful dreadlocks, carefully groomed, like wild plants in well-tended rows.

Soon after moving there, I became the Democratic precinct leader for our neighborhood, and I used to pass her house as I made my rounds. She not only had hair I loved but a glorious bright overgrown garden like one you'd find on the grounds of Clown College. One time I stopped to talk to her when she was out in her yard picking flowers, and I admired her dreads out loud. "You ought to do it," she said. "My daughter and I did it as an act of civil rights. And we could help you do it, too."

I said that sounded just great—but I knew I wasn't going to follow up. First of all, I felt it was presumptuous to appropriate a black style for my own liberation. But mostly when I thought about having dreadlocks, I felt afraid and disloyal. Dreadlocks would be a way of saying I was no longer going to play by the rules of mainstream white beauty. It meant that I was no longer going to even try and blend. It was a way of saying that I know what kind of hair I have, I know what it looks like, and I am going to stop trying to pretend it's different than that. That I was going to celebrate instead.

But I was not ready; I continued to moussify.

No one knew the effort it took to make my hair look like it hadn't taken any effort at all.

I'd pass Marlene working in her garden, and she'd look up from her work and say, "You have such beautiful hair."

"Oh, thank you," I'd say, and paw the ground.

One day she said, "I *love* your hair." And then she went on, "Picture Jesus with hair just like yours." But I couldn't, any more than I could imagine him with braces on his teeth or short hairy legs. That's how deeply I had come to believe that my hair was ugly.

On the other hand, I *could* immediately see Jesus with

dreadlocks flowing down his back. And I saw that it would be an act of both triumph and surrender to give up trying to have straighter hair. And that surrender means you get to come on over to the winning side.

But I *still* wasn't ready to do it.

Then two things happened. One was that all of a sudden I couldn't stop thinking of something Pammy said right before she died, when she was in a wheelchair, wearing a wig to cover her baldness. We were at Macy's. I was modeling a short dress for her that I thought my boyfriend would like. But then I asked whether it made me look big in the hips, and Pammy said, as clear and kind as a woman can be, "Annie? You really don't have that kind of time." And—slide trombone, bells, rim shot—I *got* it, deep in my being. While walking by Marlene's garden, Pammy's words suddenly rang through the chambers of my mind.

So I kept thinking, How much longer am I going to think about my hair more often than about things in the world that matter? I kept passing Marlene's house. She'd be out watering her crazy clown garden. We'd talk about politics, our children, and God. Then we'd talk about hair. "Call me," she'd say, "when you're ready." She knew how scared I was.

One day I said, "I think I'm getting there."

"Princess be about to *arrive*," she said.

The second thing was that right around that time, I saw *The Shawshank Redemption,* where at the end, the character played by Tim Robbins escapes from prison via the sewers after serving time for a crime he didn't commit. He emerges from the pipes of the prison into a rushing rain-swollen river, and he staggers through the current with his face turned toward the sky, his arms held up to heaven as the rains pour down.

I sat in the movie theater and cried for a while. Then I started to smile, because it occurred to me that if I were the prisoner being baptized by the torrential rain, half my mind would be on how much my bangs were going to shrink up after they dried.

I went home that night and I called Marlene. "OK, baby," I said. "I'm ready."

The next day she and her dreadlocked teenage daughter came over to my house with a little jar of beeswax, which would hold the baby dreads in place until they could start tangling themselves together into strands. Marlene sat me down in the kitchen. She and her daughter sectioned off my hair, twisted it into long strands that almost looked braided, and glued it in place with the wax. It took a couple of hours, and I was scared almost the whole time. We listened to gospel and reggae for inspiration. I cried a little— I had never let people enter into my hair weirdness with me, had never let anyone help me before, had never believed I could get free. I let them work on me, and after a while I thought of the sacredness of animals grooming each other. I felt the connection and the tenderness, the reciprocal healing offered by the laying on of hands. The two women twisted, daubed, smoothed my hair, practical and gentle at the same time; there aren't many opportunities for this left, away from the sickbed. Marlene worked with the grave sense that we were doing something meaningful—politically, spiritually, aesthetically. And her quiet daughter worked with bouncy joyful efficiency, bopping along to the reggae beat. When they were done, I looked beautiful—royal, shy, groomed. Beautiful. Strange. Mulatto.

Who will love me now? I wondered. Will anyone want to stroke my hair again? I didn't know the answer, so this act was like taking a vow of chastity. And I didn't care. I just wanted to stroke my hair myself.

The dreads are so cool: no wonder two people in Saint Louis wanted my secret. Like snowflakes, each dreadlock is different, has its own configuration, its own breadth and feel. It's like having very safe multiple personalities. It's been four years since that day Marlene and her daughter first twisted them into vines, and they have grown way past my shoulders down my back. Sometimes I wear them up, sometimes down. I used to look at people with normal white people's hair, and their bangs always stayed long and they got to hide behind that satin curtain, and I was jealous. But now my bangs are always long, too. I peered out at St. Louis from behind my dreadlocks, as through a beautiful handmade fence, in the drizzle, in the wind, in the rain.

# BABY

—————

I have a story about alchemy.

Sam and I were an hour from shore on the Sea of Cortez last year. We were on a snorkeling expedition to Seal Island, where we had gone with twenty other people to swim with the seals. Sam was the only kid, and there was only one child's wet suit, and it was just a crummy pretend wet suit. First of all, it was bright pink, which I told Sam was considered an extremely manly color in Mexico. But the main problem was that it had no arms or legs, just a torso, and it was very thin. It couldn't be very insulated. So when we anchored off Seal Rock and everyone else got in the water and began bobbing along in their thick intensely buoyant wet suits, I got a sinking sensation.

But I am old and tough, and I said a little prayer and climbed off the tailgate of the cruise boat into the frigid water. By then almost everyone else was already in the cove where the seals were lounging around on the rocks, barking like drunken guard dogs. Sam was more excited than I can remember him being in a long time. He stood there on the boat in his snorkeling mask and his manly bright pink wet suit, with his skinny little arms and legs, looking like a cross between Jacques Cousteau and Pee-Wee Herman. And then he slid into the water beside me.

God, it was cold. And the current was stronger than I had imagined; it was so hard to tread water without being moved along in the flow that I felt really afraid. It became clear that Sam would need me to hold onto him while we were in the water, whereas I had been imagining that we would swim along together side by side. But courage is fear that has said its prayers, and so I prayed and kept one arm around him and we bobbed in place for a moment as best we could. Sam is a very strong swimmer for a young boy, and finally we began swimming to the cove. Dozens of seals barked from the rocks, and we headed toward them, toward the other people who were in the water right near them. But after we'd gotten twenty feet away from the boat, Sam cried out in despair that one of his flippers had come off, and as I peered through the bottomless water I could see it below us floating downward to the depths. I almost let him go to retrieve it, but it didn't make sense to leave Sam at the surface even for an instant in his crappy pink nonbuoyant wet suit while I went after it, so I watched the flipper sink.

We bobbed together for a moment, me and my boy, and the tide was pushing us along, not toward shore but toward the sea. By then I was hearing the soundtrack of *Jaws* beginning to play, and I had to decide whether to make a break for the cove where the seals were or to head back to the boat. Sam begged that we swim toward the seals, and my head thought we could do it but my heart was afraid.

And so we headed back. I kept hoping that someone

would swim up alongside us, a big guy who was such a strong swimmer that he could accompany Sam to the cove, but no one came.

We reached the cruise boat, got out of the water, and sat on the tailgate. Sam's shoulders were hunched together, little wings in pink polyurethane, and he bit his lower lip, pretending to be interested in something way out over the horizon. And I said to God, "*Do* something—I mean, for God's sake." About five minutes later, the snorkeling guide Rafael came over to say *he'd* take Sam with him when he headed over and that if I wanted, I could head off alone. Sam gaped at me with joy, and I was only a bit worried about whether Rafael could actually swim, or had a drug problem, or a history of pedophilia. But because Sam's face had lit up again, I took a long deep breath and smiled. A few minutes later I adjusted my mask, slid off the boat, saluted Sam, and took off for the cove.

I swam ahead of Sam and Rafael to where everyone else was, looking back once or twice to locate the two of them in the water near the boat. My heart was so happy for Sam. Seals swam up quite close to me and barked and were properly silly, as they are paid to be, and it was goofy and sweet, and I bobbed along with the other people for a while and then tried to locate Sam in the water. I scanned the sea, looking for a little guy in a bright pink wet suit, but I couldn't find him anywhere.

Finally I realized that this tiny blue bundle back on the tailgate of the boat was my boy. And I knew it hadn't worked, that he hadn't been big enough to make the swim after all.

I swam back. I was panting with the effort of swimming

against the tide, and I realized it would have been terribly difficult for me to maneuver Sam back to the boat by myself. But my heart felt broken for him, and my mask got all fogged up. I climbed back on board and sat down beside him. He was wrapped in a blue towel. Someone had brought him a Coke and some tortilla chips. It turned out that he had started getting hypothermic a minute or two after getting in the water, and Rafael had brought him back to the boat. Sam was grievously disappointed but was being very brave. I was desperate to fix him, fix the situation, make everything happy again, and then I remembered this basic religious principle that God isn't there to take away our suffering or our pain but to fill it with his or her presence, so I prayed for the health simply to enter into Sam's disappointment and keep him company.

And it was about one moment later that the extraordinary happened: dozens of seals started swimming up to us. "Ahhh!" Sam cried, as the first seal bobbed a few feet away, and this time his cry was one of total amazement. And then another seal emerged a few feet away, right next to the first one, and they bobbed near each other, looking right at us with their moist doggy compassion. Sam started laughing, and I felt the moment go from cramped to very spacious. Sam cried out with laughter. The seals' heads looked like old men's bald pates that you wanted to pat. As they bobbed up and down in the water, hiding from us, then emerging again, I shook my fist at them and called out, "Hey—what d'ya think you are—a couple a comedians?" They kept swimming up to us for the next fifteen minutes, popping up out of the water like furry lightbulbs of a good idea.

After a while, all the adult humans swam back to the

boat from the cove, and the seals went under the waves, and soon we were on our way back home.

Sam and I sat side by side on the deck as we sped along on the endless blue. Then Sam leaned forward, craning his neck to see something over the side of the boat, and I thought at first he imagined he saw the seals following him out here into the ocean, or maybe their friends or cousins, notified by underwater telegraph that a disappointed kid was passing by. But it wasn't seals that he saw. Instead—God must have been in one of her show-offy moods—the next thing we knew, the boat was surrounded on both sides by dolphins, literally hundreds of dolphins leaping out of the waves everywhere you looked, in arcs like rainbows, vaulting in and out of the water like aquatic clowns. It was almost too much; I hung my head and laughed. Everyone on board was crying out in joy as more and more dolphins leapt on both sides of the boat; it was like the end of the Fourth of July when they set off every last firework they have, and a new explosion follows before the last has even disappeared.

When we were back in our room, I said, "Honey, you need to write this down so that we never forget what happened today." He didn't want to at first, as he does not really like writing very much and has a terrible time with spelling, so I had to bribe him with the promise of a virgin piña colada. Then he finally sat down and began to write. I lay on my bed pretending to read but watching him work: he is a very slow writer, looking like a thoughtful old person with arthritis and bad vision. After a while he got up from his desk to get his crayons, and then he drew a picture below his story, bending in very close to the page again, his face not more than two inches from the paper. I let him work in peace for as long as I could stand it. Then I said, "Honey, what are you drawing?"

"What do you think? I'm drawing *dol*phins."

This is the story he wrote, painstakingly, above his drawing of the dolphins leaping over our boat: "I am going to see the seals. I took a boat to see the seals but I could not make it to the shore. But they came to me. And on the ride back we saw some dolphins and it was magic to us."

So you see? Alchemy: dross to gold.

# Part Seven

# SHORE AND GROUND

Keep walking, though there's no place to get to.
Don't try to see through the distances. That's not
　for human beings.
Move within, but don't move the way fear makes
　you move.
Today, like every other day, we wake up empty and
　frightened.
Don't open the door to the study
and begin reading. Take down a musical
　instrument.

Let the beauty we love be what we do.
There are hundreds of ways to kneel and kiss the
　ground.

RUMI

# A MAN WHO
# WAS MEAN TO HIS DOG

S am and I were back at the beach near San Quentin
prison when we saw the ugliest real-life thing Sam has
ever witnessed. We had gone to the beach for just the opposite reason, of course. We went because we like to build
things and to throw sticks to our dog Sadie in the surf,
because the water washes off her fleas and soothes her skin.
Her joy is boundless, and that is great to be a part of. We
went because there are always other children for Sam to
play with, and everyone leaves me alone to read my magazines and lie in the sand with my ears open. The sound of
the surf, the big washing machine of ocean, sometimes
seems to rinse out my brain, or at any rate, it expands me
and it slows me down.

I also surprise myself by how quickly I can move there.
Many things used to make me run fast—fear, joy, ambition,
fast friends—but now the ocean is one of the few things
that can still do it: I walk along, feeling large and cautious,
only to find myself suddenly dodging a wave, fleet as a deer.
Sam hunts and gathers treasures for his sand buildings; he
studies the work at hand. I notice how phantasmagorical

people look on the beach, with the sun either right in your eyes so you can hardly make them out, or backlighting them, crowning them with light. But the other day when the man who did the ugly thing showed up, when he came walking down the wooden stairs that deposit you on this small, secluded beach, he looked plain, solid, and absolutely ordinary. A large forty-ish man in a blue flannel shirt and jeans, with a big golden retriever on a leash.

It's not that Sam had never witnessed powerful, frightening things before. For such a small person, he's already had a big life. He has stayed close to three people he's loved in the days before their deaths. He's even seen a dead body.

And we've read scary books and watched scary movies and TV shows together. He's met monsters, ghouls, and demons on the page and on the screen. There's nothing like watching *Anaconda* with your best friend or lying in bed next to your mother reading Roald Dahl, because that way you get to explore dark stuff safely. You get to laugh with it, to step out on the vampire's dance floor and take him for a spin, and then step back into your life. When you make friends with fear, it can't rule you.

But this took place a few yards away from where we stood.

Sam and I were sitting near the stairs in our swimsuits. I was wearing shorts over mine. We were watching Sadie romp with the other dogs. The man in blue flannel stood looking out over the ocean, and his big dog stood still beside him and stared straight ahead. Sadie headed over.

The two dogs touched noses, sniffed each other, kissed, cuffed. Then the man tugged gently on the leash to get his dog to walk down the beach with him. But the dog turned to Sadie one more time and took one step toward her. And the man bent down, picked up a thick stick from the ground, and smashed it into his dog's rib cage. The dog flinched big time but did not even yelp. Sam did; Sam yelped from fifteen feet away. It was absolutely stunning. All I could do was whisper, "No." Sadie looked at the dog and then tore over to us. The retriever turned to watch her go, and the man hit her again in the ribs.

Then they began walking off down the beach.

I didn't know if the man was evil or just violent. Lots of people are scary and dangerous because they are sick or stupid or powerful. Drugs and alcohol make people stupid and violent, but I don't think that necessarily makes them evil. Evil is when you choose to do such harm. So I don't know. We can't read other people's hearts. We just know what's in our own, what wrongs we are capable of, and that knowledge is terrible enough.

For instance, I desperately don't mean to do harm, but then I do. The other day I grabbed Sam's arm in a fit of rage during a controversy involving the telephone, when he was being insolent, when he was being what I believe Benjamin Spock might have called "a total little shit." I had given him three chances to do the right thing—which is to say, to do what I wanted him to do, which was to turn the ringer on the phone off. Not a big deal. And after my third entreaty, he gave me a bad look. I am not going to describe it, because he has huge angelic eyes and only weighs fifty-five pounds, and you are going to side with him. Or at least you will ask yourself, How bad could it be? Here's the answer. It was *bad;* it was Klaus Barbie, at eight years old, sneering at his mother.

In the blink of an eye, I hurt him. I misjudged how close he was to me, and I grabbed him too hard, too quickly, and with too much force. My nails actually got embedded in Sam's arm. Now, I have extremely short nails—but they went into his flesh.

The good news is that I immediately knew that I had done something wrong. I thought what most parents would think under similar circumstances: that I was unworthy and my child would be better off in foster care. I had done something Jesus would never have done. Nor do I believe that Jesus would have then picked up the phone and thrown it so hard that it left a dent in the wall. But I do believe that most of my friends would have.

I gasped and apologized. Sam froze. His mouth dropped open and he slowly lowered his gaze until it landed on his upper arm, and he gaped as if there were something sticking out of it, like an arrow from the longbow of a Japanese feudal warrior. Then he looked up at me with horror and recoiled.

By then it was almost all I could do not to laugh. I gave myself a time-out, I apologized up one side and down the other, I bowed and scraped. You try to minimize the damage you do to the innocent, even if the innocent have a tiny tendency to overdramatize things.

I knew on the beach that Jesus would have stepped in to save the dog, and he would have been loving the dog beater as he did so. He would have been seeing the dog beater's need and fear. Well, I am certainly not there yet. I myself am a bit more into blame and revenge; also, I've found that self-righteousness is very comforting. But Jesus is quite clear on this point. He does not mince words. He says you even have to love the whiners, the bullies, and the people who think they're better than you. And you have to stick up for the innocent. In Luke's Gospel, one of the two thieves being crucified beside Jesus reviles him, repeating what the mob is saying, which is that Jesus is a pretty sorry-assed Son of God if he can't even save himself. But the other thief turns to the first one, and out of his own anguish, he shows compassion to Jesus; he stands up for him. He says that Jesus hurt no one and that they should not join in hurting him. He says, in effect, "Don't kick the dog. The dog did nothing wrong."

I was frozen like in a dream when your feet weigh fifty pounds each and the danger is almost upon you. I was pretty sure that the man was not armed, but I wasn't positive. Sam began to cry. I put my arm around him, but he shook it off. "Do something," he whispered. "Do something."

First I shushed him the way I do at bedtime when in the dark, just before dropping off to sleep, he voices a fear: spiders, gremlins, kidnappers. And he quieted down, as if he believed that I was going to take care of everything now. But inside I felt as helpless as an emaciated old person with stick-figure arms, shaking her cane in the air.

I don't know how I would have felt if the dog had been a breed that I was scared of—a rottweiler, for instance. But it was a golden retriever. They're the koala bears of the dog world. And I don't know if I would have taken any further action if the abuse hadn't continued.

But then as we watched, the man, now about halfway

down the small beach, suddenly yanked his dog into a standing position and held her there. He pulled on the leash even harder so that her head tipped all the way back and her nose pointed straight into the air. It was utterly obscene. For a moment the dog hung from the leash like something on a meat hook, absolutely still.

Sam cried out again. I got to my feet, holding my breath. Behind me, another mother whom I know by sight had gotten up too. Her three children were hiding behind her, watching. She was very poor, and her children look like Dorothea Lange kids in Disney clothes. We all gawked at each other. "Stop," I quietly called to the man. I was afraid that he would come after us next. "Stop," I said again, a bit louder but still squeaky. I was trying to love him but get him to stop hurting his dog, and neither was working. Then Sam cried out really loudly again, and like Czeslaw Milosz said, his cry rang out like a pistol shot there on the beach.

I looked back at the other mother, and she nodded at me and moved forward to where I stood, and then she shouted at the top of her lungs like a warrior, "Stop! I am going to call the police now! I am going to have you arrested."

"*You* say something, Mama," whispered Sam, and this is what I said, with cold fury: "I am going to call the police too!" The man laughed. He looked insane now, no longer an ordinary guy in a flannel shirt. His eyes were bad, not hooded or shadowy but too intense, like the irises might shoot laser beams at you. He was near the wooden stairs that led to our car, and I was afraid to go past him. Then he quickly turned away and walked up the wooden stairs with his dog. After a while the six of us went up the stairs and looked around, but the man and his dog were gone.

The mother, with her brood close behind, said to us, "Let's go tell the guard at the prison gate to be on the watch for a man who is being mean to his dog." The children including Sam voiced agreement, and like the mob in *Frankenstein,* they all stormed off. I stayed behind with Sadie.

I sat down in the sand, breathless with shame and failure. God, I thought, some defender of the weak. Some freedom fighter: Joan of Arc in sunscreen. I buried my head in my hands and saw his bad eyes, saw my mousy indignation, saw the dog hanging on the invisible meat hook, saw Sam waiting for me to do something.

When Sam came back, I asked how it had gone, and he said they'd told the guard to be on the lookout for the man and that he should arrest him on sight. The guard had said he would.

"Why'd you let him get away?" Sam demanded.

"I was just so afraid, Sam. I was afraid he would hurt us."

Sam sighed with exasperation. I felt very low. Sadie, Sam, and I got up to take a walk down the beach, subdued and confused.

"Will the dog always have to live with that man?" he asked.

"Nope," I said. "I don't think so."

"Why do you think that?"

"I just do." Maybe it's wishful thinking, this snaggly faith of mine, or maybe it's Miles Davis saying, "Don't play what's there, play what's not there." If courage is not there, if the possibility of things getting better is not there, listen a little harder. God, I prayed, guide my feet, show me where to go.

I started walking faster, leaving Sam behind, suddenly wanting to get away from this cringing mouse of a mother. Well, good luck, Bubbie. I felt such a sense of my weak exposed self out in the open, out in a world that can deliver both beauty and terror in swift succession. I bent down and picked out a dozen small white agates, and held them lightly in my coward's palm. Once I saw a friend of mine throw himself under a rearing horse to save a child who'd fallen from the saddle, and I always imagined I was capable of this, too. But now I could see I wasn't. I heard Sam bossing Sadie around, and the sound of his voice startled me back to where I was. Please, I prayed. I didn't even know what I was asking for, but please.

The word *ask* caught my attention, though. I said it to myself again, and it reeled me into a memory like a fish. I was back in church the week before as one of our members stood at the pulpit telling us about how she had come to adopt her little son. She and her husband had found him through an agency called ASK, for Adopt Special Kids. First they had to fill out a questionnaire, with questions like "Could you adopt an addicted baby? A child with a terminal illness? With mild retardation? With moderate retardation? With tendencies toward violence against others?" She ticked off the list, and then she cried. Veronica stepped to her side. "God is an adoptive parent, too," she said. "And she chose us all. She says, 'Sure, I'll take the kids who are addicted, or terminal. I pick all the retarded kids, and of course the sadists. The selfish ones, the liars . . .'"

I stared at the little white agates in my hand, delicate as moon drops. The mystery of God's love as I understand it is that God loves the man who was being mean to his dog just as much as he loves babies; God loves Susan Smith, who drowned her two sons, as much as he loves Desmond Tutu. And he loved her just as much while she was releasing the handbrake of her car that sent her boys into the river as he did when she first nursed them. So of course he loves old ordinary me, even or especially at my most scared and petty and mean and obsessive. Loves me; *chooses* me.

Remembering this helped, but here is what in fact saved me: Sam came over to see what I held in my palm, glared contemptuously at my small white pebbles, and then without missing a beat slapped the bottom of my hand so that the agates scattered. He ran off down the beach, laughing with glee. It surprised me so, this small meanness, that it made me catch my breath. Boy, I thought, is *he* going to be hard to place.

When I was young I would have felt, What's the point of trying to be good if the people who aren't even *trying* get to be equally loved? Now I just picked up my pace and tried to catch up with that rotten Sam, because I don't know much of anything for sure. Only that I am loved—as is. Sam with Sadie, fifty feet ahead, turned to face me with his thumbs in his ears, waggling his fingers. It made me smile. I listened to the sound of the ocean over the sound of my own breath. I used to lie on beaches stoned and think I was hearing the sound of the universe breathing. Where else can you hear this? Hardly anywhere, although sometimes crickets have the same wonderful sound of infinity, of something lightly sawing away.

# INTO THIN MUD

I t's funny where we look for salvation, and where we actually find it. For instance, this August was such a hard month to get through. The romance I had been in ended badly. My heart was broken, and my head was just barely inhabitable. Then my darling Mary Williams died. She was eighty-six, but I thought she would live forever, bring us Baggies of dimes for the rest of our lives, sitting near the doorway at church crying, "Yes, Lord, thank you, thank you." I saw her a few hours before she died, at a convalescent home where she'd been expected to recover from the flu. The woman in the next bed cried out for some food, for a nurse, a visitor, a glass of water, anything. Someone had braided Mary's sparse gray hair into two thin braids just above her ears, like a young girl's. I said, "We worship a God of healing, Mary," and she said, "Yes, Lord, thank you, thank you." And then she died that evening. I think of her many times a day. The Baggies of dimes that she gave us still sit on bookshelves all over the house. In her open casket, she looked like a god, napping. But mostly I see her alive, smiling at us at the back of the church. I see her praying. I see her face appear in my mind, I also see the words of Langston Hughes in an old hardcover my father kept in his study:

> *The night is beautiful,*
> *So the faces of my people.*
>
> *The stars are beautiful,*
> *So the eyes of my people.*
>
> *Beautiful, also, is the sun.*
> *Beautiful, also, are the souls of my people.*

Only a week or so later, a relative I love very much was diagnosed with Alzheimer's. I felt alternately rubbery and empty, like sometimes I was landing on the Swiss cheese, sometimes on the holes.

I cried every day for a week or so, and felt a bit better. Then smaller things started going wrong, too. We ran out of money. Sam went and grew himself his first sty. Someone took a picture of him in a tie-dyed T-shirt, and he looked squinty and half blind, like it was still the sixties but the drugs were beginning to wear off. I bounced a check. Veronica took off for a week, and most of my friends who could be counted on to listen quietly and make me laugh were also on vacation. Sam's sty grew worse. Then the final straw: the car began to backfire with some regularity; pedestrians whipped their heads around when we passed, mistaking the sound for gunshots. Also—hardly worth mentioning—the engine kept running when you turned off the key.

I called my friend John, who was so sad for me and Sam

about Mary dying that he sighed again and again. Then he said that as far as the car was concerned, if you have a problem you can solve by throwing money at it, you don't have a very interesting problem. I hung my head, then dropped Sam off with my brother Steve, and took my car in for a tune-up.

They needed to keep the car overnight, but they lent me a huge Blues Brothers car with a great sound system, and it was so beautifully atrocious that it gave me a new lease on life. I roared out of the rental car lot and—bam—right into bumper-to-bumper traffic.

I thought, That's it, I'm going to throw myself under the wheels of the car. I'm going to run over my own head. But I couldn't even do *that* because I couldn't get up any speed. If you ran over your head in this gridlock, you probably wouldn't even end up dead, and your hair would be all fucked up.

So I just went home, with my big purple car and a box of See's Bordeaux. When I was a kid and my father got depressed, we all frantically tried to pump him out of it. The theory was that if Dad was OK, it would be like Reaganomics: there would be trickle-down, and everyone's needs would be met. But if Dad was not OK, we were all doomed. So this has always been my first line of attack against a slump: start pumping.

I ate a few chocolates and felt more animated. Then I crashed and was just as sad as I'd been before, but fatter and tired.

The next morning I stayed in bed quite late, not wanting to get up. I remembered lying in bed as a child, pretending to have paralyzed legs as the result of my heroic effort to save a baby from a kidnapper, or fire, or wolves. I figured that if you had suffered a wound or handicap in an act of self-sacrifice, people would not only see how badly you felt but would also believe that you were worthy of tender care. So I was lying in bed trying to drag myself into a sitting position when my friend Neshama called. She suggested we go for a hike. I could not think of a single thing I felt less like doing. A hike? And me in my condition? But Neshama seems to think I am worthy of tender care even when I am at my most ridiculous, so I said I would go.

Neshama and I go back to my Bolinas days, twenty-five years ago. We've been through births, deaths, estrangements, confusions, and just about everything life can deal out, but have maintained our friendship through it all. Part of our bond is having had fuzzy-haired bookworm childhoods. Also she is one of the few people I know who can tolerate a lot of silence and stillness; they are central to her spirituality, as is the joy she finds in music and dance. She loves God in the guise of kindness and nature, although she calls God "Howard," as in "Our Father, who art in heaven, Howard be thy name."

On this particular morning, I put on the nicest possible clothes in an effort to raise my spirits. I wore a white linen blouse, and sandals, and lipstick. An hour later Neshama and I were walking down a hillside toward a marsh we had spotted from the road. From up above it looked fertile and abandoned, surrounded by nondescript suburban houses and anonymous buildings, like Mesopotamia accidentally deposited in the midst of a military complex. You felt that no one living there was even aware of the marsh, that they and their buildings had turned their backs on it. It also looked quite boggy, like maybe you should be wearing waders instead of sandals, but I figured, what the hell—this must be where we were going because this was where we were.

We left the road where the hillside dipped down into the marsh, a brackish tidal channel with lots of red pickerel-weed and cattails. A dirt path ran alongside it. There were snowy egrets in the channel, with star-shaped yellow feet. Everything was very quiet. Even though the freeway was not far away, you could hear only white noise and soft rustle, as if the marsh had sucked up all the other sound. Sometimes you'd hear a grackly crow noise or one of the egrets, who tend to sound as if they need oiling.

We walked along the path until we got to a thin ribbon of water flowing out from the channel toward the bay. I stopped, remembering the Sunday not long ago when Mary Williams testified. She brought a long pole and an old housedress draped over her arm, blue, faded, and frayed. At the point when Veronica would normally begin the sermon, she instead asked Mary to stand and tell us her baptism story. Mary rose with the help of the women who sat beside her, and while she spoke, they spotted her, like you would a gymnast.

She put the housedress on over her church clothes to represent the robe she wore to be baptized in. She tugged it into place and picked up her pole. Then, her voice as soft and rough and Southern as biscuits, she told of the day seventy years before when she stepped into the Mississippi

River to be baptized. She lived in Louisiana. She was not yet in her teens and her mother had been dead for years. On the morning of her baptism, she went with her father and brother to the river. There was a ring of poles sticking out of the water near the shore. The deacons had walked out in the river that morning, feeling around on the muddy floor with their poles until they found a solid patch of riverbed. Then they stuck the sticks into the mud, forming a circle in which the people could safely stand with their pastor and be baptized.

She tapped the linoleum at our church like a blind woman with a white stick, the eyes of that girl still right there in that walnut face.

And suddenly at the marsh with Neshama, the ground and vegetation at our feet began to get a little watery, and then we began to hear sucking noises, swampy quicksandy sucking noises, and pretty soon my overpriced walking sandals had been swallowed up by mud.

We moved as quickly as possible through the bog to drier ground on the other side. Then we stared down at our muddy shoes, and we started to laugh. It's just *mud*, we realized. It washes off. Mary Williams got baptized in it. So we tromped on until the path came smack-dab up to a stumpy wet slope, with ratty little shrubs growing out of it. The path picked up again at the top. There was nothing to do but to scale it, and I use "scale" loosely here, since the slope was only about three feet tall.

"Let me help you there, little lady," I said. "I'll go up first and then give you a hand." So I planted a foot on the muddy dune, grasped a root, and would have pulled myself up the hill nicely if the root had held. But it didn't. It pulled up out of the slope, and I slid down on my butt to the wet ground. Both of us started to laugh. Then I got up and tried again, like Sir Edmund Hillary's dauntless fiancée, and this time I made it up. Planting one foot firmly on the driest ground I could find, I reached back down for Neshama's hand.

"Is this a good idea?" she asked. "Are you braced?"

"Yes," I insisted, and pulled her toward me, and she lifted up off the ground and moved upward a couple of feet, until I started sliding back down toward her and we both landed noisily on our butts in the mud.

I looked at her. She was wearing a blue linen dress and ballet slippers because she was going to work from here, and she was utterly covered with silt. I started to laugh. It was odd to be so old and to have gotten so muddy, to have such dirty drawers and no angry parents around, and no more face to save.

I was laughing so hard that I felt maniacal and not at all sure that I wasn't about to cry. But I felt like air was bubbling into a place inside me that hadn't been getting much lately. I looked at Neshama's ballet slippers. "Boy," I said, "are you going to get it when Mom sees you," and she nodded. I couldn't stop laughing. It made me feel helpless in the best possible way. The laughter rose from way below, from below my feet, from underneath my butt in the mud.

Finally we stopped laughing, wiped our eyes, sighed, gathered some composure. We sat there silently for a long time. There were egrets on a telephone wire above us, looking down on the smorgasbord of wiggly jumpy things that lived in the shallow water; maybe birds like to get up high so they can see if there are food patterns in the swamp. And there were two blackbirds on the wire, sitting on either side of the egrets like bookends. The air smelled of dry grasses—warm smells, a little like a Laundromat. Then I let my head drop down narcoleptically and closed my eyes for a while.

Against the sparkly black screen behind my eyes, all these people appeared, like people in a come-as-you-are fashion show, strangers to each other but beloved by me. There were all the sick little kids we know, and all the friends who had died—Mimi, and Ken Nelson, and Mary Williams—and the old people in my family and church who had grown so suddenly frail, and the man with whom I used to be in love and who used to be in love with me. And I thought to myself, "Well, no wonder you're this sad." The silence of the marsh was so profound that it could have been the flip side of the singing in my church. Just last Sunday the people of St. Andrew had sung the old spiritual, "Go Down, Moses," a cappella because the pianist was gone, and a bunch of people were crying, singing very loudly with their eyes closed, and the singing of that cry of a song was a wonderful form of communion. How come you can hear a chord, and then another chord, and then your heart breaks open?

When Neshama and I finally got up to go, I was still sad, but better. This is the most profound spiritual truth I know: that even when we're most sure that love can't conquer all, it seems to anyway. It goes down into the rat hole with us, in the guise of our friends, and there it swells and comforts. It gives us second winds, third winds, hundredth winds. It struck me that I have spent so much time trying to pump my way into feeling the solace I used to feel in my parents' arms. But pumping always fails you in the end. The truth is that your spirits don't rise until you get *way* down. Maybe it's because this—the mud, the bottom—is where it all rises from. Maybe without it, whatever rises would fly off or evaporate before you could even be with it for a moment. But when someone enters that valley with you, that mud, it somehow saves you again. At the marsh, all that mud and one old friend worked like a tenderizing mallet. Where before there had been tough fibers, hardness, and held breath, now there were mud, dirt, water, air, mess—and I felt soft and clean.

# ALTAR

S am and I were on the beach at San Quentin on the morning of his eighth birthday. He was having a party that afternoon at our best friends' house, and four of his friends from school were invited, but he'd agreed to come with me to the beach until then. It gave me a great excuse not to write—it was my kid's birthday, for God's sake. The truth, though, was that I'd hardly written in weeks, and then only pitiful little stream-of-consciousness writing exercises, like Job's wife trying to get the *Artist's Way* to work. I couldn't remember the point anymore; a lot of rewards had come my way, but I felt like a veteran greyhound at the racetrack who finally figures out that she's been chasing mechanical bunnies: all that energy, and it's not even a real rabbit. It was an awful predicament, to be so tired of doing what I do and, at the same time, worried that the jig was going to be up this time for sure, that I wasn't going to be *allowed* to do it anymore. That the authorities were going to call and say I'd blown my chance to be one of the writers—but they'd found me a new job, at the Laundromat. I was going to be the anxious woman who hands out change: "Here, here's some quarters. Don't use that machine, it overflows! Hey! That man's using your basket!"

But Sam at eight is fantastic, utterly magic. He's so much bigger than he was last year. His legs are nearly longer than mine, and he styles his hair now before he goes to school, moussifies it into a punk look sometimes, and other times slicks it back until, as he put it, "it looks fancy." His spiritual views are changing; sometimes he says he doesn't believe in only Jesus now. He says, "I believe in all the gods now," but that may be just to torture me. I'm not that concerned yet, but let me get back to you on this when he starts leaving *Eck Speaks!* pamphlets around for me to find.

Half the time he's so gentle and sweet that grown-ups smile and shake their heads at such a good child. With infinite patience, he has taught a number of children to ride two-wheelers over the years, and he gives them flattened bottle caps as medals of encouragement when they fail. But he can be terribly unfriendly with me, and he's got this new toughness, this teenage impersonation that he pulls out from time to time with varying effect. For instance, he told me not long ago, with rather nonchalant sadism, "No one thinks you're funny." Mostly this facade is pretty touching, though. I recently dropped him off for a couple of hours with our fourteen-year-old friend Rory, who is the coolest boy you've ever met, and Sam immediately went into this unconscious adolescent parody, a fifty-five pound Sean Penn, all slouchy tics and slanted eyes and bored derision. When I picked him up later at Rory's, he slouched out to the car with his bottom lip hanging down as if a lit cigarette were dangling from it, and as we drove off, Sam sneered,

"He thinks he's so cool, but he doesn't even have the Disney Channel."

So there we were, my eight-year-old boy and I, building a something or other. It had begun as a castle but had morphed into a woolly-mammoth-shaped birthday altar with turrets. We spelled out his name on the sand in the center of the structure with letters made from tiny broken white shells. We stuck feathers, seaweed, beach glass, and shells in the turrets and humps.

Sam really has a gift for making things out of next to nothing. He has magic in those little monkey fingers. He sees things spacially. His last teacher, after expressing some concern about his handwriting, said, "He makes such amazing things out of . . . of . . . of," and I said, "Garbage?," and she said, "Yes!" He walks along looking in dirt and carpets and corners for discarded bits of metal or plastic, packaging, string, and then like somebody knitting very quickly, he fiddles these things into little contraptions. For instance, with a plastic container that had once held snack cheese and crackers, and a strand of maroon embroidery thread, a large bent paper clip, a popsicle stick, and a little ball of foil, he made an apparatus for hypnotizing animals, with a spring-lock closure so that any bad guys who stole it could never get it to work.

Sometimes I have a knee-jerk concern that he has so little interest in school. At the end of second grade, one of the mothers said, "Gee, he doesn't go much for homework, does he?," and I wanted to scream, "No, but he makes *inventions,* you dumb slut, out of *garbage.* While your kid is an obsequious little Type A suck."

I realize I may be the least bit sensitive.

Sam and I had built huge ramparts around our castle and had dug a moat to keep out the aliens and bad guys. He thinks and talks and dreams about bad guys all the time—also, monsters and dangerous animals. He looked so lost—and so found—in his work on the beach, his vision so clear and focused, while here I was in the middle of an emotional kaleidoscope. What a year: so much love, so many deaths and setbacks. It was all too much. I had begun to feel like when you're a kid, and you and your friends pretend to be outrunning hot lava and then all of a sudden it turns out that it has caught up to you and is swirling around your ankles. I looked over at Sam. He had just covered a turret with cannonballs of round beach pebbles. He still looks like a wood sprite, although definitely a more manly wood sprite.

We were working away side by side until Sam saw some sandpipers and got up to race down to the water, flapping his wings at them. They all flew away. Sam is built just like my father, whom we always called "Old Birdlegs." But he tans well. My father's legs were as pale as the moon.

The sandpipers landed fifty feet away, and Sam returned. He got back to work. But we both kept glancing up at them. They look so absurd; they're well adapted but you'd never know just by looking at them. You have to see them in action, right on the edge, trying to scrabble out a living. Now Sam left them alone and bounded around looking for useful items. I listened to the sandpipers' cries of alarm, took in their spindly legs, their masks of pure white, their features patterned like speckled brown eggs.

Walking and digging, walking and digging along the shore, poking their long pointed beaks into the sand, hoping there's food.

They're very naked. There's such intensity in them, too, the intensity of the moment—like the gypsies, they can't drift off or they might die, and because of this quality of necessary attention, they have a lovely precision, dancing a kind of comical ballet.

"You're not even going to believe what I just scored," Sam shouted on his return, cocky and pumped up like a very short boxer before a fight. He had things hidden behind his back and brought out his hands to reveal several really cruddy-looking clothespins. "Do you have a pen?" he asked breathlessly, and I did, in the back pocket of my jeans.

Sam took my pen and drew in faces, mustaches, hair. He took a bit of black pipe cleaner that was stuck in a turret and fashioned a machine gun out of it for one of the clothespin men. He surrounded his castle with the men he has nightmares about, men with guns, men who will hurt or save him; and he surrounded his castle with monsters made of Styrofoam and seaweed. His art springs out of bubbling underground necessity, as if he's somehow dipping himself into the river that gave him life; he's making dream material visible. I watched him carefully. He was making art because he has to, and because he's brave enough to try and make contact, right there on the edge of madness, where he dreams.

"We have to go," I told him. The party at our friends' house was going to start in an hour or so.

"No!" he wailed. "We can't. What about . . . our creation? We can't just leave it here. We have to stay and protect it. We've worked so hard on it! The waves will come and wash it away."

"Honey," I said, "it was never meant to be permanent. You must have known the tide would come back in."

He thought about this for a minute. "I'm going to kick it all over, then," he said. "And I *hate* you," he added. "And I hate *everything.*"

I didn't say anything. He walked away from me and the altar, world weary, shuffling with dejection, head down. Sam, I wanted to explain, making the altar was a way to celebrate, to honor you today. The fact that it's going to wash away heightens how wonderful our *making* it was. The altar didn't hold as much animating spirit as our *making* it did, the gathering, the choices. It's like: We made it, we love it—oops, it's gone. But the best part is still here.

Of course I didn't say any of this, and he didn't in fact kick his birthday altar over. Some time later he came back to where I lay and asked if we could stay just a while more. I said yes, sure, and smoothed some sand off his face with my fingertips. He let me, and then walked off again. I lay back down and closed my eyes, and I guess I must have fallen asleep. Because later still he was tugging at my sleeve until I opened my eyes and sat up. He had his fists balled up, concealing something, and he wanted me to guess which hand the secret was in. I tapped the left fist, and he unfurled his fingers to reveal an oval of soft pink beach glass.

"Wow," I said, picking it out of his small palm. If you'd

seen my face, you would have thought he'd just given me a Spanish doubloon. He stood there watching me with a long sideways look, his face turned slightly away, pleased with my reaction but determined not to show it. The glass was polished from the sea, and I put it in the pocket of my shorts. "Thank you," I said, and he shrugged. Then he actually chucked me under the chin, like one of my uncles used to do, and ran off again to the shore.

The waves haven't come for my smooth glass yet. In the meantime, it is right here in the front pocket of the jeans I am wearing now. I reach into my pocket for it a lot; it helps me write in some mysterious way I don't at all understand. But what I want to say is, happy birthday, Sam, Samuel John Stephen Lamott. And traveling mercies, too. I can't help but say again what I said on the beach that day, in a whisper this time and without even being exactly sure to whom I'm saying it: Thank you. Thank you. Thank you.

# ACKNOWLEDGMENTS

I could not write my books without the love and brilliant input of Neshama Franklin and John Kaye. It is as simple as that. David Talbot, my wonderful editor at Salon Magazine (www.salonmagazine.com), gave me ideal conditions in which to write early drafts of these pieces. Nancy Palmer Jones is a truly collaborative copyeditor, who has greatly improved my last five books. I would be inconsolable without my editor, Robin Desser, and Altie Karper, who is always there. My brother Stevo and my son Sam help everything in the world make sense to me. Three wise priests, Monsignor Terrence Richey, Father Tom Weston, and the Reverend William Rankin, spent hours with me explaining religious principles, and making me laugh. Beth Ashley, Beverly Bastian, Betty McKegney, Gertrud Schleiger, Louise Teather, and my mother Nikki Lamott often helped me with the details of Marin County history. Clara MacNamee was my marine and geology consultant, Deirdre English helps me to understand politics better than anyone else. She might be the smartest woman on earth. Jane Vandenburgh is the most wonderful and generous writer of all. I benefit in daily and myriad ways from my friendship with the late great Don Carpenter. And Pat Nissan was the visionary who first helped me understand that it was possible to get a lounge chair in heaven, near heaping bowls of Gulf shrimp, which is where she is now, and forevermore.

# PERMISSIONS
# ACKNOWLEDGMENTS

Grateful acknowledgment is made to the following for permission to reprint previously published material:

*Broadway Books and Coleman Barks:* Excerpt from *The Illuminated Rumi* by Coleman Barks and illustrated by Michael Green. Copyright © 1997 by Coleman Barks and Michael Green. Reprinted by permission of Broadway Books, a division of Random House, Inc. and Coleman Barks.

*Grove/Atlantic:* Excerpt from "Later Fragment" from *A New Path to the Waterfall* by Raymond Carver. Copyright © 1989 by the Estate of Raymond Carver. Reprinted by permission of Grove/Atlantic, Inc.

*Alfred A. Knopf, Inc.:* Excerpt from "Thanks" from *The Rain in the Trees* by W. S. Merwin. Copyright © 1988 W. S. Merwin. Reprinted by permission of Alfred A. Knopf, Inc.

*Alfred A. Knopf, Inc., and Faber and Faber Ltd.:* Excerpt from "Thirteen Ways of Looking at a Blackbird" from *Collected Poems* by Wallace Stevens. Copyright © 1923 and renewed 1951 by Wallace Stevens. Reprinted by permission of Alfred A. Knopf, Inc., and Faber and Faber Ltd.

*Alfred A. Knopf, Inc., and Harold Ober Associates Incorporated:* Excerpts from "Dream Dust and "My People"

# ABOUT THE AUTHOR

ANNE LAMOTT is the author of *Operating Instructions: A Journal of My Son's First Year* and *Bird by Bird: Some Instructions on Writing and Life*, as well as the novels *Hard Laughter, Rosie, Joe Jones, All New People,* and *Crooked Little Heart*. A past recipient of a Guggenheim Fellowship, she lives with her son, Sam, in Northern California.